THE LIBRARY OF TRADITIONAL WISDOM

The Library of Traditional Wisdom has as its aim to present a series of works founded on Tradition, this term being defined as the transmission, over time, of permanent and universal truths, whose written sources are the revealed Scriptures as well as the writings of the great spiritual masters.

This series is thus dedicated to the *Sophia Perennis* or *Religio Perennis* which is the timeless metaphysical truth underlying the diverse religions, together with its essential methodological consequences.

It is in the light of the *Sophia Perennis,* which views every religion "from within," that may be found the keys for an adequate understanding which, joined to the sense of the sacred, alone can safeguard the irreplaceable values and genuine spiritual possibilities of the great religions.

LIGHT ON THE ANCIENT WORLDS

FRITHJOF SCHUON

Translated by Lord Northbourne

Second Edition

WORLD WISDOM BOOKS

ERRATA

Page 8, line 1. 'of "age of the Gods" ' *should read* 'of the "age of the Gods" '

Page 27, line 6. For 'Churches' *read* 'churches'

Page 29, line 31. For 'Māyā' *read* '*Māyā*'

Page 31, line 26. For 'themselves disavowed it' *read* 'disavowed it themselves'

Page 40, line 36. For 'of' *read* 'on'

Page 43, line 28. For 'know they' *read* 'know what they'

Page 56, line 31. For 'effective *read* 'affective'

Page 57, line 13. For 'prayer' *read* 'Prayer'

Page 61, line 36. For '*charitas*' read '*caritas*'

Page 61, line 37. For 'χάριτας' *read* 'ἀγάπη'

Page 69, line 36. Dashes should be hyphens, i.e. 'man-intelligence' and 'man-will'

Page 71, line 32. 'Prakriti' *should be* '*Prakriti*'

Page 89, line 22. (Aẓ-Zāhir) *should be* (*Az-Ẓāhir*)

Page 95, line 19. For 'manifestation *Māyā* '*read* 'manifestation of *Māyā*'

Page 114, line 20. For 'mutiplication' *read* 'multiplication'

Page 115, line 11. For 'sources' *read* 'source'

Page 120, line 21. For 'his own age' *read* 'the world'

Page 120, line 26. For 'facts' *read* 'fact'

Page 121, line 34. For 'sants' *read* 'saints'

Page 122, line 21. For '(lā rahbāniyah fī'l-islām)' *read* '(*lā rahbāniyah fī'l-islām*)'

Page 129, line 29. For 'whole' *read* 'while'

Page 144, line 6. For 'or admit more than one "tradition" ' *read* 'or have "traditions" '

Page 144, line 21. For 'controlled' *read* 'operated'

CONTENTS

CHAPTER I

THE ANCIENT WORLDS IN PERSPECTIVE

T HE whole existence of the peoples of antiquity, and
of traditional peoples in general, is dominated by two
presiding ideas, the idea of Centre and the idea of
Origin. In the spatial world we live in, every value is related
back in one way or another to a sacred Centre, to the place
where Heaven has touched the earth; in every human world
there is a place where God has manifested Himself to spread
His grace therein. Similarly for the Origin, the quasi-timeless
moment when Heaven was near and when terrestrial things
were still half-celestial; but the Origin is also, in the case of
civilizations having a historical founder, the time when God
spoke, thereby renewing the primordial alliance for the branch
of humanity concerned. To conform to tradition is to keep
faith with the Origin, and for that very reason it is also to be
situated at the Centre; it is to dwell in the primordial Purity
and in the universal Norm. Everything in the behaviour of
ancient and traditional peoples can be explained, directly or
indirectly, by reference to these two ideas, which are like land-
marks in the measureless and perilous world of forms and of
change.

It is a "mythological subjectivity" of this kind that makes
understandable, for example, the imperialism of ancient civilizations, for one cannot simply put everything down to the
"law of the jungle", even though that law may in fact be
biologically inevitable and to that extent legitimate; one must
also take into account, and even, since human beings are concerned, give precedence to, the fact that each ancient civilization can be said to live on a remembrance of the lost Paradise,
and that it believes itself—in so far as it is the vehicle of an
immemorial tradition or of a Revelation that restores the "lost

word"—to be the most direct branch of "age of the Gods".
It is therefore in every case "our own people" and no other
who perpetuate primordial humanity from the point of view
both of wisdom and of the virtues; and this outlook, it must
be recognized, is neither more nor less false than the exclusivism of the religions nor, on the purely natural plane, than
each *ego's* experience that he alone is "I". There are many
peoples who do not call themselves by the name by which
they are known to others; they call themselves simply "the
people" or "men"; other tribes are unbelievers, they have
separated themselves from the main stem. Such a point of
view is, broadly speaking, that of the Roman Empire as well
as of the confederation of the Iroquois.

The purpose of the ancient imperialism was to spread an
"order", a condition of equilibrium and stability that conforms to a divine model, and is in any case reflected in nature,
notably in the planetary world. The Roman emperor, like the
monarch of the Celestial Middle Kingdom, wields his power
thanks to a "mandate from Heaven". Julius Caesar, holder
of this mandate and "divine man" (*divus*),[1] was conscious of
the range of his mission; as far as he was concerned, nothing
had the right to oppose it; Vercingetorix was in his eyes a
sort of heretic. If the non-Roman peoples were regarded as
"barbarians", it is precisely because they were outside the
"order"; they manifested, from the point of view of the *pax
romana*, disequilibrium, instability, chaos, perpetual menace.
In Christianity (*corpus mysticum*) and Islam (*dar-al-islam*)
the theocratic essence of the imperial idea is clearly apparent;
without theocracy there could be no civilization worthy of
the name. So true is this that the Roman emperors, in the
midst of the pagan break-up and from the time of Diocletian,
felt the need to divinize themselves or to allow themselves to
be divinized, while improperly attributing to themselves the
title of conquerors of the Gauls descended from Venus. The
modern idea of "civilization" is not without relation, historically speaking, to the traditional idea of "empire"; but the
"order" has become purely human and wholly profane, as
the notion of "progress" proves, since it is the very negation of

8

any celestial origin; "civilization" is in fact but urban refinement in the framework of a wordly and mercantile outlook, and this explains its hostility to virgin nature as well as to religion. According to the criteria of "civilization", the contemplative hermit—who represents human spirituality and at the same time the sanctity of virgin nature—can be no better than a sort of "savage", whereas in reality he is the earthly witness of Heaven.

These considerations lead naturally to a few observations on the complexity of Authority in Western Christianity. The emperor, as opposed to the Pope, incarnates temporal power; but more than that, he also presents, by virtue of his pre-Christian but nevertheless celestial origin,[2] an aspect of universality, whereas the Pope is identified by his function with the Christian religion alone. The Muslims in Spain were not persecuted until the clergy had become too powerful in comparison with the temporal power; the temporal power, which appertains to the emperor, represents in this case universality or "realism", and therefore "tolerance", and therefore also in the nature of things a certain element of wisdom. This ambiguity in the imperial function—of which the emperors were conscious to a greater or less extent[3]—partly explains what may be called the traditional disequilibrium of Christianity; and one might well think that the Pope had recognized this ambiguity—or this aspect of superiority paradoxically accompanying an inferiority—by prostrating himself before Charlemagne after his coronation.[4]

Imperialism can come either from Heaven or merely from the earth, or again from hell; however that may be, what is certain is that humanity cannot remain dissociated into independent tribes like fragments of dust; the bad ones would inevitably fling themselves at the good, and the result would be a humanity oppressed by the bad, and so the worst of all imperialisms. What may be called the imperialism of the good constitutes therefore a sort of inevitable and providential preventive war; without it no great civilization is conceivable.[5] It may be argued that all this does not get us away from human imperfection, and that is very true; the present argu-

9

ment, far from preaching a chimerical superhuman goodness, gives full weight to the fact that man remains always man whenever collectivities with their interests and their passions come into the picture; the leaders of men are obliged to take account of that fact, unpleasant though it be to those "idealists" who consider that the "purity" of a religion consists in committing suicide. This leads to a truth which is all too often lost sight of by believers themselves: it is that religion, in so far as it is manifested collectively, necessarily relies on something to support it in one way or another, without for that reason losing anything either of its doctrinal and sacramental content or of the impartiality they imply; for the Church is one thing as a social organism and another as the repository of the Divine Spirit, which remains by definition outside the entanglements and servitudes of human nature both individual and collective. Attempts to modify the terrestrial roots of the Church—roots that are largely held in balance by the phenomenon of sainthood—end by debasing the very essentials of religion, in conformity with the "idealist" prescription whereby the surest way of healing the patient is to kill him. In our days, in default of the ability to raise human society to the level of the religious ideal, religion is lowered to the level of that which is humanly accessible and rationally realizable, but which is nothing from the point of view either of our integral intelligence or of our possibilities of immortality. The exclusively human, far from being able to maintain itself in equilibrium, always ends by sinking down to the sub-human.

*　　*　　*

In traditional worlds, to be situated in space and time is to be situated in a cosmology and in an eschatology respectively; time has no meaning save in relation to the perfection of the origin and the maintenance of that perfection, and in view of the final breaking up that casts us almost without transition at the feet of God. If as time went on there were sometimes developments which could be taken to have been progressive when isolated from the whole—in the formulation of doctrine for example, or especially in art, which needs time and experience to ripen—this does not imply that tradition can be regarded as having become different or better, but on the contrary that it wants to remain wholly itself, or to "become what it is"; or in other words, that traditional humanity wants to manifest or to externalize at a particular level something that it carries within itself and is in danger of losing, and the danger increases as the cycle unfolds, the cycle inevitably ending in decline and Judgment. It is therefore our increasing weakness, and therewith the risk of forgetfulness and betrayal, which more than anything else obliges us to externalize and to make explicit things that were at the beginning included in an inward and implicit perfection. Saint Paul had no need either of Thomism or of Cathedrals, for all profundities and all splendours were in himself, and all around him in the sanctity of the primitive community. And this, so far from supporting iconoclasts of all kinds, refutes them completely; more or less late epochs—the Middle Ages for example—are faced with an imperious need for externalizations and developments, exactly as the water from a spring, if it is not to be lost on its way, needs a channel made by nature or by the hand of man; and just as the channel does not transform the water and is not meant to do so—for no water is better than spring water—so the externalizations and developments of the spiritual patrimony are there, not to change that patrimony, but to transmit it as integrally and as effectively as possible.

A particular ethnic genius may prefer to emphasize one aspect or another—with every right to do so, and all the more freely because every ethnic genius comes from Heaven—but its function cannot be to falsify the primordial intentions; on the contrary, the vocation of this genius consists in making those intentions as transparent as possible to the mentality it represents. On the one hand there is symbolism, which is as rigorous as the laws of nature and no less diverse than they, on the other hand there is the creative genius which in itself is free as the wind, but is nothing without the language of Truth and of the Symbols providentially at hand, and is never hurried nor arbitrary. That is why it is absurd to declare, as is so often done today, that the Gothic style, for example, expresses its "times" and that for the Christians of "today" it constitutes an "anachronism"; that to "follow the Gothic" is "plagiarism" or "pastiche", and that we must create a style that conforms to "our own times", and so on. To do so is to ignore the fact that Gothic art was situated in space before becoming the retrospective incarnation of an epoch; in order to escape from the specifically Gothic idiom, the Renaissance ought to have begun by understanding it, and that understanding would have implied grasping its intrinsic nature and its timeless character; and if the Renaissance had understood it, there would have been no reason to escape from it, for it goes without saying that the abandonment of an artistic idiom must have a motive other than incomprehension and lack of spirituality. A style expresses both a spirituality and an ethnic genuis, and these two factors cannot be improvised. A collectivity can pass from one formal language to another in so far as an ethnic predominance or a spiritual flowering makes it necessary to do so, but it can in no case attempt to change its style on the pretext that it is giving expression to a "period", and therefore to relativity, and consequently to the very thing that calls in question the absolute values that are the sufficient reason of every tradition. The predominance of the Germanic influence, or the rise of the creative consciousness of the Germanic peoples, acting in concert with a predominance of the emotional side of Christianity, spontaneously gave rise to the formal language which later came to be called "Gothic".

The French who created the cathedral did so as Franks and not as Latins, though this in no way prevented them from manifesting their Latinity at other levels, or even within the framework of their Germanity; nor must it be forgotten that, spiritually speaking, they were Semites like all Christians, and that it is this mixture—with the addition of a Celtic contribution—which produced the genius of the mediaeval West. Nothing in our days justifies the desire for a new style; if men have become "different", they have done so in an illegitimate manner and through the operation of negative factors, by way of a series of Promethean betrayals such as the Renaissance; the illegitimate and the anti-Christian obviously cannot produce a Christian style nor can they make a positive contribution to any such style. It could be argued that our epoch is so important a fact that it is impossible to ignore it, since one is obliged to take unavoidable situations into account; that is true enough, but the only conclusion to be drawn from it is that we ought to go back to the most sober and the most severe of mediaeval forms, to fit in with the spiritual distress of our epoch; we ought to quit our anti-religious "times" and reintegrate ourselves with a religious "space". An art that does not express the changeless and does not want to be itself changeless is not a sacred art; the cathedral-builders did not want to create a new style—had they wanted to they could not have done so—but they wanted to impart, without any "research", to the changelessness of the Romanesque a slant that seemed to them more ample and more sublime or more explicit; they wanted to crown and not to abolish. Romanesque art is more static and more intellectual than Gothic art, and the Gothic is more dynamic and more emotional than the Romanesque; but each style expresses spontaneously and without Promethean affectations the changelessly Christian.[6]

*   *   *

When one is speaking of ancient or traditional peoples it is important not to confuse healthy and integral civilizations with the great paganisms—for the term is justified here —of the Mediterranean and the Near East, of whom Pharaoh and Nebuchadnezzar have become the classic incarnations and conventional images. What strikes one first in these "petrified" traditions of the world of the Bible is a cult of the massive and the gigantic, as well as a cosmolatry often accompanied by sanguinary rites, not forgetting a development to excess of magic and of the arts of divination. In civilizations of this kind the supernatural is replaced by magic, and the here and now is divinized while nothing is offered for the hereafter, at least in the exoteric field which in fact overwhelms everything else; a sort of marmorean divinization of the human is combined with a passionate humanization of the Divine; potentates are demigods and the gods preside over all the passions.[7]

A question that might arise here is the following: how was it that these old religions could deviate into paganism and then become extinct, whereas a similar destiny seems to be excluded in the case of the great traditions that are alive today in the West and in the East? The answer is that traditions having a prehistoric origin are, symbolically speaking, made for "space" and not for "time"; that is to say, they saw the light in a primordial epoch when time was still but a rhythm in a spatial and static beatitude, and when space or simultaneity still predominated over the experience of duration and change. The historical traditions on the other hand must take the experience of "time" into account and must foresee instability and decadence, since they were born in periods when time had become like a fast-flowing river and ever more devouring, and when the spiritual outlook had to be centred on the end of the world. The position of Hinduism is intermediate in the sense that it has the faculty, exceptional in a tradition of the primordial type, of rejuvenation and adaptation; it is thus both prehistoric and historic and realizes in its own way the miracle of a synthesis between the gods of Egypt and the God of Israel.

To return to the Babylonians: the lithoidal character of this type of civilization cannot be explained in terms of a tendency to excess alone; it may also be explained in terms of a sense of the changeless; it is as if they had seen the primordial beatitude evaporating and had therefore wanted to build a fortress, with the result that the spirit was stifled instead of being protected; seen from this angle the marmorean and inhuman side of these paganisms looks like a titanic reaction of space against time. From this point of view the implacability of the stars is paradoxically combined with the passions of bodies; the stellar vault is always present, divine and crushing, while an overflowing life takes the place of a terrestrial divinity. From another point of view, many of the characteristics of the civilizations of antiquity are explained by the fact that in the beginning the celestial Law was of an adamantine severity while at the same time life still retained something of the celestial. Babylon lived falsely on this sort of recollection; but there existed none the less, at the very heart of the most cruel paganisms, mitigations that can be accounted for by changes in the cyclical atmosphere. The celestial Law becomes less demanding as the end of our cycle approaches; Clemency grows as man becomes weaker. The acquittal by Christ of the adulterous woman carries this meaning—apart from other meanings no less admissible—and so does the intervention of the angel in the sacrifice of Abraham.

Nobody would think of complaining of the mitigation of moral laws; it is, however, proper to consider it, not in isolation, but in its context, because it is the context that reveals its intention, its range and its value. In reality the mitigation of moral laws—to the extent that it is not illusory—can represent an intrinsic superiority only on two conditions, namely, firstly that it confers a concrete advantage on society, and secondly that it be not obtained at the cost of that which gives meaning to life. Respect for the human person must not open the door to a dictatorship of error and baseness, to the crushing of quality by quantity, to general corruption and the loss of cultural values, for if it does so it is, in relation to the ancient tyrannies, but an opposite extreme and not the norm. When humanitarianism is no more than the expression of an over-valuation of the human at the expense of the Divine, or of the crude fact at the expense of the truth, it cannot possibly be counted as a positive acquisition. It is easy to criticize the "fanaticism" of our ancestors when one has lost the very notion of a truth that brings salvation, or to be "tolerant" when one despises religion.

Whatever the customs of the Babylonians[8] may have been, it must not be forgotten that certain kinds of behaviour depend largely on circumstances and that man always remains a sort of wildling, at least in the "Iron Age". The conquerors of Peru and of Mexico were no better than Nebuchadnezzar,

Cambyses, or Antiochus Epiphanus, and one could find analogous examples in the most recent history. The religions can reform the individual man with his consent—and it is never the function of religion to make up for the absence of that consent—but nobody can bring about a fundamental change in that "thousand-headed hydra" which man is collectively, and that is why nothing of the kind has ever been the intention of any religion; all that the revealed Law can do is to dam up the egoism and the ferocity of society by canalizing its tendencies more or less effectively. The goal of religion is to transmit to man a symbolic image, but one that is equated to the reality that concerns him, according to his real needs and his ultimate interests, and to provide him with the means to surpass himself and to realize his highest destiny; that destiny can never be of this world, our spirit being what it is. The secondary goal of religion is to realize, with the main goal in view, a sufficient equilibrium in the life of the collectivity, or to safeguard, within the framework of the natural malice of men, a maximum of spiritual opportunity; if on the one hand society must be protected against the individual, on the other hand the individual must be protected against society.

There is endless talk about "human dignity", but it is rather too often forgotten that *"noblesse oblige"*; dignity is invoked in a world that is doing everything to empty it of its content, and thus to abolish it. In the name of an indeterminate and unconditional "human dignity", unlimited rights are conceded to the basest of men, including the right to destroy all that goes to make our real dignity, that is to say, everything on every plane that attaches us in one way or another to the Absolute. Without doubt truth obliges one to stigmatize the excesses of the artistocracy, but one can see no reason at all why it should not also confer a right to judge excesses that are anything but aristocratic.

*   *   *

In those ancient times, so much decried in our days, the rigours of earthly existence, including the wickedness of men,

16

were on the whole accepted as an inexorable fatality, and their abolition was, with good reason, believed to be impossible. In the midst of the trials of life, those of the hereafter were not forgotten, and it was admitted also that man has need of suffering as well as of pleasure here below, and that a collectivity cannot maintain itself in the fear of God and in piety by contact with nothing but the pleasurable;[9] such was the thinking of the *élite* at all levels of society. Miseries, of which the deep-seated cause is always the violation of a celestial norm as well as indifference towards Heaven and our ultimate destiny, are there to restrain the greedy illusions of men, rather in the same way as the carnivores are there to prevent the herbivores from degenerating or multiplying to excess; everything is related to universal equilibrium and to the homogeneity of the world; a consciousness of this is part of the fear of God. In the light of this elementary wisdom, a progress conditioned by spiritual indifference, and by an idolatry of well-being taken as an end in itself, cannot constitute a real advantage, that is to say, an advantage proportioned to our total nature and to our immortal kernel. That is evident enough; nevertheless, even in the most "believing" circles, people go so far as to claim that technical progress is indisputably a good thing, and that it is therefore a blessing even from the point of view of faith. In reality modern civilization gives in order to take : it gives the world but takes away God; it is this that compromises even its gift of the world.

In these days there is a stronger tendency than ever to debase happiness to the level of economic satisfaction—which is anyhow unattainable in the face of an indefinite creation of artificial needs and a sordid mystic of envy—but there is one thing that is completely lost sight of when this outlook is projected into the past, and that is that a traditional craft and a contact with nature and with natural things are factors essential to human happiness. These are just the factors that disappear in industrialism, which enforces all too often, if not always, an inhuman environment and as it were "abstract" manipulations, movements with no intelligibility and no soul,

17

all carried out in an atmosphere of frigid cunning. We have arrived, beyond all possibility of argument, at the antipodes of what the Gospel means when it enjoins us to "become as little children" and to "take no heed for the morrow". The machine transposes the need for happiness on to a purely quantitative plane, having no relation to the spiritual quality of work; it takes away from the world its homogeneity and its transparence and cuts men off from the meaning of life. More and more the notion of intelligence is debased into conformity with what the machine demands, and our capacity for happiness is measured by what it offers; since we cannot humanize the machine, we are obliged, by the force of a certain kind of logic at least, to mechanize man; having lost contact with the human, we prescribe what man is and what happiness is.

A barren argument, some people will say. This affords an opportunity, at the risk of becoming involved in one more digression, to stigmatize a misuse of language or of thought which is met with almost everywhere and is particularly typical of contemporary "dynamism". An argument is not "barren" or "fruitful", it is true or false. If it is true, it is all that it ought to be, and it could not then in any case be "barren" in itself; if it is false, the question of its eventual "fruitfulness" does not arise, for error cannot be otherwise than harmful or indifferent, according to the domains and the proportions involved. One must react against this tiresome tendency to substitute a utilitarian and subjective choice —or a moral choice—for an intellectual and therefore objective judgment, and to put the "constructive" in place of the true, as if truth were not positive in its nature, and as if anything useful could be done without it.[10]

An analogous misuse is commonly made of the notion of "charity". It appears that in response to a new orientation of ideas, Catholics must "understand" their contradictors according to "charity" instead of judging them with "egoism" and regarding them as adversaries. Here again there is a confusion between totally unrelated domains. In reality the situation is very simple : faced by a common danger, oppositions existing among those who are threatened by it are in practice diminished; to describe the danger as common implies that the opposition between the aggressor and the victims is eminently greater than the oppositions that divide the victims one from another; but in the absence of the aggressor or of his threat, the original oppositions retain all their virulence or at least their actuality. In other words, an outward opposition becomes inward in the view of the rivals when they are faced by a third opposition that conflicts with their common nature; this is a logical or "physical" datum free from any sentimentality. From a certain point of view the contradiction between Catholicism and Protestantism is essential and irreducible; from another point of view, both Catholics and Protestants believe in God, in Christ, and in the future life; to say that Protestants are not in any connection adversaries of Catholics, or the other way round, is just as illogical as to pretend that they have no ideas or interests in common. For centuries at the heart of Western Europe practically the only confessional antagonism was that produced by the Reformation, Protestantism being opposed from its birth and by definition to the ideas and the interests of the Roman Church; they were what is called "enemies", even when no animosity as between individuals is presumed,[11] and whatever the partisans of the new "charity" may say. But in our days the situation has changed, and that rather abruptly, in the sense that the common interests and ideas of all Christians, and even of all religious believers of all kinds, find themselves threatened by a new power, that of a materialist and atheist scientism, whether it be of the "left" or of the "right". It is evident that in such circumstances not only do the factors of unity prevail in certain respects over those of division, but also that the dangers which one confession represents in the eyes of another —or one religion in the eyes of another[12]—become less or disappear. To talk all of a sudden, and loudly, of a "charity" which the Church is alleged to have lost sight of for a thousand years or more, and to contrast it with the "narrowness" or the "egoism" of a "past age" is a very bad joke on the part of the Catholics; and in any case it is unconscious hypocrisy, like other sentimentalities of the same order, all the more because this so-called "charity" is fostered by a certain dislike of theology and a desire to suppress, or to "neutralize", all doctrinal, and thus all intellectual, elements. In other days an agreement was an agreement and a disagreement was a disagreement, but in our days one pretends to "love" all that one does not know how to suppress, and one makes it appear that one believes that our fathers were neither intelligent enough nor charitable enough to be able to distinguish between ideas and men, and to be capable of loving immortal souls independently of the errors that affect them. To the objection that the masses were and are incapable of grasping these subtleties, the answer is that the same applies the other way round : if too many subtleties are thrust upon the masses the result will be confusion of ideas and indifference; the average man is made like that, and there is no difficulty in seeing that he is so. However that may be, to preach to a confessional adversary is to try to save his soul, it is therefore to love him in a certain way; to fight an adversary is to protect one's own religion, and is therefore to fight for God. Our times, so imbued in some respects with "understanding" and with "charity"—though these words too often serve as masks for unintelligence, complacency and cold calculation—our times excel beyond all question in not understanding and not wanting to understand what the men of earlier times thought and did, men who were in many cases a hundred times better than their detractors.

We will now leave these digressions and return to more retrospective matters that are in some respects less "up to date".

*　　*　　*

The knight of former days had to choose between two things : the risk of death and the renunciation of the world. The greatness of responsibility, of hazard or of sacrifice coincides with the quality of "nobility"; to live nobly is to live in company with death, with a death either carnal or spiritual. The knight had no right to lose sight of the fissures in existence; being obliged to view things from an eminence, he could never be far from their nothingness. Furthermore, if one is to be able to rule others, one must know how to rule oneself; an internal discipline is the essential qualification for the functions of chief, of judge, or of warrior. True nobility, which cannot in any case be the monopoly of a function, implies a penetrating consciousness of the nature of things and at the same time a generous giving of the self, consequently it excludes idle fancies no less than meanness.[13]

The courts of princes must reflect the quality of a centre, a hub, a summit, but they must not degenerate—as happened all too often—into a false paradise; the shimmering dream of Versailles was already a betrayal, a firework without purpose and without greatness. Courts are normally focal points of science, art and magnificence; it is evident that they must not exclude austerity of habits, very much the reverse, for asceticism is not opposed to elegance any more than virtue is opposed to beauty or beauty to virtue. Royal festivities are legitimate—or tolerable—by virtue of their spiritual symbolism and their political and cultural radiation, and by virtue of the "divine right" of Caesar; court festivities are the "liturgy" of an authority conferred by the "mandate of Heaven". But all that is nothing—let it be repeated once more—if the princes, or the nobles generally, do not preach by their example in all respects, and in the first place in their fear of God, without which nobody has the right to demand respect and obedience. This is one of the chief functions of the holders of authority and of power; the fact that in too many cases they have not been faithful to it is what has brought about their fall; they have forgotten Heaven, and so they have been forgotten by it.

But there is still something more to be said. All manifestations of princely splendour, whatever their symbolism and their artistic value—and whether they are necessary or not—always carry within themselves the metaphysical seeds of their own ruin. Strictly speaking, the hermit alone is absolutely legitimate, for man was created alone and dies alone. The hermit as such is specifically mentioned because he represents a principle and is therefore a symbol, but without confusing an outward isolation with the holy solitude which, for its part, can and must find a place in all human situations. Social virtues are nothing without this solitude and, by themselves they engender nothing lasting, for before acting one must be; it is this quality of being that is so cruelly lacking in the men of today. It is forgetfulness of our solitude in God—of this terrestrial communion with celestial dimensions—that brings in its train all human failings as well as all earthly calamities.

These considerations could also be expressed in the following way: in a traditional climate men live as if they were suspended from an ideal and invisible prototype, with which they are seeking to be reunited as their particular situations permit and according to their sincerity and their vocation. Every man ought to be a contemplative and to live among men like a hermit as far as vocation is concerned; "worldliness" is an anomaly, strictly speaking; it has only become illusorily normal on account of the fall—or the successive falls—of man or of groups of men. We are made for the Absolute, which embraces all things and from which none can escape; this truth is marvellously well presented in the monotheistic religions in the alternative between the two "eternities" beyond the grave. Whatever may be the metaphysical limitation of this concept, it provokes none the less in the soul of the believer an adequate presentiment of what the human condition is outside the terrestrial matrix and in face of the Infinite. The alternative may be insufficient from the point of view of total Truth, but it is psychologically realistic and mystically efficacious; many lives are squandered away and lost for the single reason that a belief in hell and in paradise is lacking.

The monk or the hermit, and every contemplative, though he be a king, lives as if in the antechamber of Heaven;[14] on this very earth and in his carnal body he has attached himself to Heaven and enclosed himself in a prolongation of those crystallizations of Light that are the celestial states. That being so one can understand how monks or nuns can see in the monastic life their "Paradise on earth"; they are at rest in the Divine Will and wait in this world below for nothing but death, and in so doing they have already passed through death; they live here below as if in Eternity. The days as they succeed one another do but repeat always the same day of God; time stops in a single blessed day, and so is joined once more to the Origin which is also the Centre. And it is this Elysian simultaneity that the ancient worlds have always had in view, at least in principle and in their nostalgia; a civilization is a "mystical body", it is, in so far as that is possible, a collective contemplative.

*   *   *

These considerations lead to the crucial problem of obedience, so essential in normal civilizations and so little understood in modern ones, which nevertheless admit it without cavil when it is a question of collective discipline, though it be sometimes to the detriment of the most elementary spiritual rights. Obedience is in itself a means to interior perfection, on condition that it is wholly bounded by religion, as is the case in all traditional worlds. Within those bounds, man must in some way or another obey someone or something, it may be only the Sacred Law and his own conscience if he is a prince or a pontiff; nothing and nobody is independent of God. The subordination of women, children, inferiors and servants falls into place quite normally in the system of multiple obediences that makes up a religious society; a dependence with respect to another may be a hard fate, but it always has a religious meaning, like poverty which, no less than dependence, carries a similar significance in its very nature. From the point of view of religion, the rich and the independent are by no means by definition the happy ones; ease and freedom are indeed elements of happiness in such a society, but they are only so, always from the point of view of religion, in connection with piety and in so far as they play a part in it; and this brings us back to the adage *"noblesse oblige"*. When piety exists apart from material well-being and impiety is on the contrary allied to it, true happiness is attributable to pious poverty and not to impious wealth; it is pure calumny to pretend that religion as such, or through its institutions, has always been on the side of the rich. On the one hand, religion is there to transform those human beings who are willing to allow themselves to be transformed, but on the other hand, religion must take men as they are, with all their natural rights and their collectively ineradicable faults, on pain of not being able to survive in the world of men.

In the same line of thought, one more observation must be made, whether it be agreeable or not. It is that a society as such, or by virtue of the mere fact that it exists, represents nothing of value; this implies that the social virtues are nothing in themselves, and apart from the spiritual context that orients them towards our final goal; to pretend that such is not the case is to falsify the very definition of man and of the human. The supreme Law is the perfect love of God— a love that must engage our whole being, as the Scripture says—and the second Law, that of love of the neighbour, is "like unto" the first. Now "like unto" does not mean "equivalent to", and still less "superior to", but "of the same spirit"; Christ means that the love of God manifests itself extrinsically by love of the neighbour, wherever there is a neighbour; that is to say that we cannot love God while hating our fellow-creatures. In conformity with our full human nature, love of the neighbour is nothing without the love of God, the one draws all its content from the other and has no meaning without it; it is true that to love the creature is also a way of loving the Creator, but on the express condition that its foundation be the direct love of God, otherwise the second Law would not be the second but the first. It is not said that the first law is "like unto" or "equal to" the second, but that the second is equal to the first, and this signifies that the love of God is the necessary foundation and *conditio sine qua non* of all other charity. This relationship can be discerned—sometimes imperfectly but always recognizably in principle—in all traditional civilizations.

No world is perfect, but every human world must possess the means to perfection. A world has value and legitimacy according to what it does for the love of God and for nothing else; and by "love of God" is meant first the choice of Truth and then the direction of the will: the Truth that makes us conscious of an absolute and transcendant Reality—at once personal and suprapersonal—and the will that attaches itself to it and recognizes in it its own supernatural essence and its ultimate end.

NOTES

(1) "See the man, see him of whose promised coming thou hast so often heard, Caesar Augustus, son of a God, who will found anew the Golden Age in the fields where Saturn reigned of old, and who will extend his empire even over the Garamantes and the Indians" (Aeneid VI, 791–795). Caesar prepared a world for the reign of Christ. Note that Dante placed the murderers of Caesar in the deepest hell, together with Judas. Cf. *Divus Julius Caesar,* by Adrian Paterson, in *Etudes Traditionnelles,* June, 1940.

(2) Dante has no hesitation in citing this kind of superhuman origin in support of his doctrine of imperial monarchy.

(3) The position is clear beyond doubt in the case of Constantine as well as of Charlemagne.

(4) There is a curious relationship, it may be mentioned in passing, between the imperial function and the part played by the court jester, and this relationship seems to be associated with the fact that the costume of jesters, as well as that of certain emperors, was adorned with little bells, like the sacred robe of the High Priest. The role of the jester was originally that of saying in public what nobody else could allow himself to say, thus introducing an element of truth into a world constrained by unavoidable conventions; and this function, whether one likes it or not, is reminiscent of gnosis or of esoterism because of the fact that in its own way it shatters "forms" in the name of the spirit that "bloweth where it listeth". Folly alone can allow itself to enunciate cruel truths and to touch idols, precisely because it stands apart from certain human relationships, and this proves that, in this world of theatrical artificiality which is society, the pure and simple truth is madness. This is no doubt why the function of the court jester succumbed in the end to the world of formalism and hypocrisy: the intelligent fool ended by giving place to the buffoon, who very soon became tedious and disappeared.

(5) It might seem that the spiritual decadence of the Romans must have been prejudicial to an imperial mission, but that is not so, because the Romans possessed those qualities of strength and generosity—or of tolerance—that are necessary for this providential function. Rome persecuted the Christians because they threatened every-

thing that, in the eyes of the ancient world, made Rome what it was; if Diocletian could have foreseen the edict of Theodosius abolishing the Roman religion, he would still not have acted otherwise than he did.

(6) The so-called "advanced" architecture of our epoch lays claim to being "functional", but it is only so in part, and in a wholly exterior and superficial way, since it ignores functions that are not material or practical: it excludes two elements essential to human art, namely, symbolism, which is as strict as truth, and the joy at once contemplative and creative that is gratuitous like grace. A purely utilitarian "functionalism" is perfectly inhuman in its premisses and in its results, for man is not an exclusively avid and cunning creature, he cannot really be at ease inside the mechanism of a clock. So true is this that functionalism itself feels the need to dress itself up in new fantasies, which are most paradoxically justified by the shameless assertion that they are part of the "style".

(7) The cases of Greece and of Egypt were much less unfavourable than those of post-Sumerian Mesopotamia or of Canaan; the Greeks, like the Egyptians, possessed a complete eschatology and a relatively influential esoterism. The Pharaoh of the Bible seems to represent an isolated case rather than a type; according to Clement of Alexandria, Plato owed much to the sages of Egypt. The least unfavourable case among the pre-monotheistic civilizations of the Near East was perhaps that of Persia, whose ancient tradition still survives in our days in India in the form of Parsism. The Muslims have a special respect for Cyrus, as well as for Alexander the Great, and they venerate as a saint the wife of Pharaoh.

(8) Their name is used here as a symbol, because of the associations of ideas evoked by the very word "Babylon", and not in order to make out that they were necessarily the worst of all men, nor yet the only bad ones.

(9) Mencius did not hesitate to say, in speaking of society: "Grief and trouble bring life, whereas prosperity and pleasure bring death." This is the quasi-biological law of rhythms expressed in lapidary terms, or the law of the pruning of trees and bushes. It also constituted the great argument of the Red Indians in face of the temptations and constraints of the white civilization.

(10) A truth can be inopportune having regard to circumstances or to the insufficiency of a particular subject, or category of subjects, or it can be situated at an insignificant level and have no scope; but it goes without saying that normal possibilities and logical relationships are here in view.

(11) As for the unbelievers, they were not sufficiently dangerous to the Protestants, nor even to the Catholics, to be the cause of a sentimental reconciliation between the two confessions.

(12) Pius XII therefore had logic on his side when he said that the crusades were "family quarrels". If the Moslem menace was not a factor of union between Christians divided by schisms and heresies, it is because the menace was external and not internal as scientism is. Under the Arab or Turkish domination, Christians remained Christians, whereas scientism empties the Churches even in Christian countries. In the nineteenth century, the first lay government of Greece could find nothing better to do than to close several hundred convents, which had been untouched by the Moslems.

(13) Nothing is more false than the conventional opposition between "idealism" and "realism", which insinuates in general that the "ideal" is not "real", and inversely; as if an ideal situated outside reality had the smallest value, and as if reality were always situated on a lower level than what may be called an "ideal". Anyone who holds this view is thinking in a quantitative and not in a qualitative mode. The current meaning of the terms is here in view, and not their specifically philosophical signification.

(14) It is in an analogous sense, but superior in the degree of existence to which it relates, that the Paradise *Sukhavati* is represented as surrounded by a golden thread; it is as if it were suspended from *Nirvana*, and it is thus the joyful prison which wards off suffering and is open only in the direction of total Freedom.

CHAPTER II

IN THE WAKE OF THE FALL

IN antiquity and in the Middle Ages man was "objective" in the sense that his attitude was still largely determined by "objects",[1] by objects on the plane of ideas as well as by objects of the senses; he was very far from the relativism of modern man who impairs objective reality by reducing it to accidents of nature lacking in significance and in symbolic quality; and he was equally far from a "psychologism" which calls in question the value of the subject, the knower, and thus in effect destroys the very idea of intelligence. To speak of "objects on the plane of ideas" is not a contradiction, since a concept, while it is evidently a subjective phenomenon in so far as it is a mental phenomenon, is at the same time, like every sensory phenomenon, an object in relation to the subject who takes cognizance of it; truth comes in a sense from outside, it is offered to the subject who may accept it or not accept it. Held fast as it were to the objects of his knowledge or of his faith, ancient man was little disposed to grant a determining role to psychological contingencies; his inner reactions, whatever their intensity, were related to an object and thereby had in his consciousness a more or less objective cast. The object as such—the object envisaged in all its objectivity—was the real, the basic, the immutable thing, and in grasping the object, he had hold of the subject; the subject was guaranteed by the object. This is, of course, always the case with many men, and in certain respects even with every sane man; but the aim here—at the risk of seeming to propound truisms—is to indicate, despite the fact that it can only be done approximately, the outlines of points of view that are in the nature of things complex. In any case, to be too easily satisfied by attention to the subject is to betray the object; the men of old would have had the impression of denaturing or losing the object if they had paid too much attention to the subjective pole of consciousness. It was only from the time of the Renaissance that the European became "reflexive", and so in a certain way subjective; it is true that such a reflexivity can in its turn have a perfectly objective quality, just as an idea received from without can have a subjective character owing to some bias of interest or feeling in the subject, but this aspect of the matter is not relevant here; what is relevant is that at the Renaissance man began to analyse mental reflections and psychic reactions and thus to be interested in the "subject" pole to the detriment of the "object" pole; in becoming "subjective" in this sense, he ceased to be symbolist and became rationalist, since reason is the thinking *ego*. It is this that explains the psychological and descriptive tendencies of the great Spanish mystics, tendencies which have been wrongly taken as evidence of a superiority and as a kind of norm.

This transition from objectivism to subjectivism reflects and repeats in its own way the fall of Adam and the loss of Paradise; in losing a symbolist and contemplative perspective, founded both on impersonal intelligence and on the metaphysical transparency of things, man has gained the fallacious riches of the *ego*; the world of divine images has become a world of words. In all cases of this kind, heaven—or a heaven—is shut off from above us without our noticing the fact and we discover in compensation an earth long unappreciated, or so it seems to us, a homeland which opens its arms to welcome its children and wants to make us forget all lost Paradises; it is the embrace of *Māyā,* the sirens' song; Māyā, instead of guiding us, imprisons us. The Renaissance thought that it had discovered man, whose pathetic convulsions it admired; from the point of view of laicism in all its forms, man as such had become to all intents and purposes good, and the earth too had become good and looked immensely rich and unexplored; instead of living only "by halves" one could at last live fully, be fully man and fully on earth; one was no longer a kind of half-angel, fallen and exiled; one had become a whole being, but by the downward path. The Reformation, whatever certain of its tendencies may have been, had as an overall result the relegation of God to Heaven—to a Heaven henceforth distant and more and more neutralized—on the pretext that God keeps close to us "through Christ" in a sort of biblical atmosphere, and that He resembles us as we resemble Him. All this brought with it an apparently miraculous enrichment of the aspect of things as "subject" and "earth", but a prodigious impoverishment in their aspect as "object" and "Heaven". At the time of the Revolution of the late eighteenth century, the earth had become definitely and exclusively the goal of man; the "Supreme Being" was merely a "consolation" and as such a target for ridicule; the seemingly infinite multitude of things on earth called for an infinity of activities, which furnished a pretext for rejecting contemplation and with it repose in "being" and in the profound nature of things; man was at last free to busy himself, on the hither side of all transcendence, with the discovery of the terrestrial world and the exploitation of its riches; he was at last rid of symbols, rid of metaphysical transparence; there was no longer anything but the agreeable or the disagreeable, the useful or the useless, whence the anarchic and irresponsible development of the experimental sciences. The flowering of a dazzling "culture" which took place in or immediately after these epochs, thanks to the appearance of many men of genius, seems clearly to confirm the impression, deceptive though it be, of a liberation and a progress, indeed of a "great period"; whereas in reality this development represents no more than a compensation on a lower plane such as cannot fail to occur when a higher plane is abandoned.

Once Heaven was closed and man was in effect installed in God's place, the objective measurements of things were, virtually or actually, lost. They were replaced by subjective measurements, purely human and conjectural pseudo-values, and thus man became involved in a movement of a kind that cannot be halted, since, in the absence of celestial and stable values, there is no longer any reason for calling a halt, so that in the end a stage is reached at which human values are replaced by infra-human values, up to a point at which the very idea of truth is abolished. The mitigating circumstances in such cases—for they are always present, at any rate for some individuals—consist in the fact that, on the verge of every new fall, the order then existing shows a maximum of abuse and corruption, so that the temptation to prefer an apparently clean error to an outwardly soiled truth is particularly strong. In a traditional civilization, the mundane element does all it can to compromise in the eyes of the majority the principles governing that civilization; the majority itself is only too prone to be worldly, its worldliness is not however aristocratic and light-hearted, but ponderous and pedantic. It is not the people who are the victims of theocracy, it is on the contrary theocracy that is the victim, first of aristocratic worldlings and finally of the masses, who begin by being seduced and end in revolt. The European monarchs of the nineteenth century made almost desperate efforts to dam the mounting tide of a democracy of which they had already, partially and despite themselves, become representatives. But these efforts were doomed to be vain in default of the one counterweight that could have re-established stability, and that could only be religion, sole source of the legitimacy and the power of princes. They fought to maintain an order in principle religious, but the forms in which this order was presented themselves disavowed it; the very apparel of kings, and all the other forms among which they lived, proclaimed doubt, a spiritual "neutralism", a dimming of faith, a bourgeois and down-to-earth worldliness. This was already true, to a lesser degree, in the eighteenth century, in which the arts of dress, architecture and craftsmanship expressed, if not exactly democratic tendencies, at least a worldliness lacking in greatness and strangely insipid. In this incredible age all men looked like lackeys—the nobles all the more so for being nobles—and a rain of rice-powder seemed to have fallen on to a world of dreams; in this half-gracious and half-despicable universe of marionettes, the Revolution merely took advantage of the previous suicide of the religious out-

31

look and of greatness, and could not but break out; the world
of wigs was much too unreal. Analogous remarks, suitably
attenuated to conform to eminently different conditions,
apply to the Renaissance and even to the end of the Middle
Ages; the causes of the descent are always the same when
seen in relation to absolute values. What is sometimes called
the "tendency of history" is only the law of gravity.

To state that the values of ancient man were celestial and
static, amounts to saying that man then still lived "in space";
time was merely the contingency that corroded all things; in
the face of that contingency values that are so to speak
"spatial", that is, permanent by virtue of their intemporal
finality, had always to assert themselves anew. Space symbolizes origin and immutability; time is the decadence which
carries us away from the origin while at the same time lead-
ing us towards the Messiah, the great Liberator, and towards
the meeting with God. In rejecting or losing celestial values,
man became the victim of time; in inventing machines which
devour duration man has torn himself away from the peaceful-
ness of space and thrown himself into a whirlpool from which
there is no escape.

The mentality of today seeks in fact to reduce everything
to categories connected with time; a work of art, a thought,
a truth have no value in themselves and independently of any
historical classification, but their value is always related to
the time in which they are rightly or wrongly placed; everything is considered as the expression of a "period" and not as
having a timeless and intrinsic value; and this is entirely in
conformity with modern relativism, and with a psychologism
or biologism that destroys essential values. In order to "situ-
ate" the doctrine of a scholastic, for example, or even of a
Prophet, a "psychoanalysis" is prepared—it is needless to emphasize the monstrous impudence implicit in such an attitude
—and with wholly mechanical and perfectly unreal logic the
"influences" to which this doctrine has been subject are laid
bare. There is no hesitation in attributing to saints, in the
course of this process, all kinds of artificial and even fraudu-
lent, conduct; but it is obviously forgotten, with satanic incon-

sequence, to apply the same principle to oneself, and to explain one's own supposedly "objective" position by psycho-analytical considerations; sages are treated as being sick men and one takes oneself for a god. In the same range of ideas, it is shamelessly asserted that there are no primary ideas; that they are due only to prejudices of a grammatical order—and thus to the stupidity of the sages who were duped by them—and that their only effect has been to sterilize "thought" for thousands of years, and so on and so forth; it is a case of expressing a maximum of absurdity with a maximum of subtlety. For procuring a pleasurable sensation of important accomplishment there is nothing like the conviction of having invented gunpowder or of having stood Christopher Columbus' egg on its point. This philosophy derives all it has in the way of originality from what, in effect, is nothing but a hatred of God; but since it is impossible to abuse directly a God in whom one does not believe, one abuses Him indirectly through the laws of nature,[2] and one goes so far as to disparage the very form of man and his intelligence, the very intelligence one thinks with and abuses with. There is however no escape from the immanent Truth: "The more he blasphemes", says Meister Eckhart, "the more he praises God".

Mention has already been made of the passage from objectivity to reflexive subjectivity—a phenomenon pointed out by Maritain—and at the same time the ambiguous character of this development has been emphasized. The fatal result of a "reflexivity" that has become hypertrophied is an exaggerated attention to verbal subtleties which makes a man less and less sensitive to the objective value of formulations of ideas; a habit has grown up of "classifying" everything without rhyme or reason in a long series of superficial and often imaginary categories, so that the most decisive—and intrinsically the most evident—truths are unrecognized because they are conventionally relegated into the category of things "seen and done with", while ignoring the fact that "to see" is not necessarily synonymous with "to understand"; a name like that of Jacob Boehme, for example, means theosophy, so "let's turn over". Such propensities hide the distinction between the "lived vision" of the sage and the mental virtuosity of the profane "thinker"; everywhere we see "literature", nothing but "literature", and what is more, literature of such and such a "period". But truth is not and cannot be a personal affair; trees flourish and the sun rises without anyone asking who has drawn them forth from the silence and the darkness, and the birds sing without being given names.

In the Middle Ages there were still only two or three types of greatness: the saint and the hero, and also the sage; and then on a lesser scale and as it were by reflection, the pontiff and the prince; as for the "genius" and the "artist", those glories of the lay universe, their like was not yet born. Saints and heroes are like the appearance of stars on earth; they reascend after their death to the firmament, to their eternal home; they are almost pure symbols, spiritual signs only provisionally detached from the celestial iconostasis in which they have been enshrined since the creation of the world.

* * *

Modern science, as it plunges dizzily downwards, its speed increasing in geometrical progression towards an abyss into which it hurtles like a vehicle without brakes, is another example of that loss of the "spatial" equilibrium characteristic of contemplative and still stable civilizations. This criticism of modern science—and it is by no means the first ever to be made—is made not on the grounds that it studies some fragmentary field within the limits of its competence, but on the grounds that it claims to be in a position to attain to total knowledge, and that it ventures conclusions in fields accessible only to a supra-sensible and truly intellective wisdom, the existence of which it refuses on principle to admit. In other words, the foundations of modern science are false because, from the "subject" point of view, it replaces Intellect and Revelation by reason and experiment, as if it were not contradictory to lay claim to totality on an empirical basis; and its foundations are false too because, from the "object" point of view, it replaces the universal Substance by matter alone, either denying the universal Principle or reducing it to matter or to some kind of pseudo-absolute from which all transcendence has been eliminated.

In all epochs and in all countries there have been revelations, religions, wisdoms; tradition is a part of mankind, just as man is a part of tradition. Revelation is in one sense the infallible intellection of the total collectivity, in so far as this collectivity has providentially become the receptacle of a manifestation of the universal Intellect. The source of this intellection is not of course the collectivity as such, but the universal or divine Intellect in so far as it adapts itself to the conditions prevailing in a particular intellectual or moral collectivity, whether it be a case of an ethnic group or of one determined by more or less distinctive mental conditions. To say that Revelation is "supernatural" does not mean that it is contrary to nature in so far as nature can be taken to represent, by extension, all that is possible on any given level of reality, it means that Revelation does not originate at the level to which, rightly or wrongly, the epithet "natural" is normally applied. This "natural" level is precisely that of physical causes, and hence of sensory and psychic phenomena considered in relation to those causes.

If there are no grounds for finding fault with modern science in so far as it studies a realm within the limits of its competence—the precision and effectiveness of its results leave no room for doubt on this point—one must add this important reservation, namely, that the principle, the range and the development of a science or an art is never independent of Revelation nor of the demands of spiritual life, not forgetting those of social equilibrium; it is absurd to claim unlimited rights for something in itself contingent, such as science or art. By refusing to admit any possibility of serious knowledge outside its own domain, modern science, as has already been said, claims exclusive and total knowledge, while making itself out to be empirical and non-dogmatic, and this, it must be insisted, involves a flagrant contradiction; a rejection of all "dogmatism" and of everything that must be accepted *a priori* or not at all is simply a failure to make use of the whole of one's intelligence.

Science is supposed to inform us not only about what is in space but also about what is in time. As for the first-named category of knowledge, no one denies that Western science has accumulated an enormous quantity of observations, but as for the second category, which ought to reveal to us what the abysses of duration hold, science is more ignorant than any Siberian shaman, who can at least relate his ideas to a mythology, and thus to an adequate symbolism. There is of course a gap between the physical knowledge—necessarily restricted—of a primitive hunter and that of a modern physicist; but measured against the extent of knowable things, that gap is a mere millimetre.

Nevertheless, the very precision of modern science, or of certain of its branches, has become seriously threatened, and from a wholly unforeseen direction, by the intrusion of psychoanalysis, not to mention that of "surrealism" and other systematizations of the irrational; or again by the intrusion of existentialism, which indeed belongs strictly speaking not so much to the domain of the irrational as to that of the unintelligent.[3] A rationality that claims self-sufficiency cannot fail to provoke such interferences, at any rate at its vulnerable points such as psychology or the psychological—or "psychologizing"—interpretation of phenomena which are by definition beyond its reach.

It is not surprising that a science arising out of the fall—or one of the falls—and out of an illusory rediscovery of the sensory world should also be a science of nothing but the sensory, or what is virtually sensory,[4] and that it should deny everything which surpasses that domain, thereby denying God, the next world and the soul,[5] and this presupposes a denial of the pure Intellect, which alone is capable of knowing everything that modern science rejects. For the same reasons it also denies Revelation, which alone rebuilds the bridge broken by the fall. According to the observations of experimental science, the blue sky which stretches above us is not a world of bliss, but an optical illusion due to the refraction of light by the atmosphere, and from this point of view, it is obviously right to maintain that the home of the blessed does not lie up there. Nevertheless it would be a great mistake to assert that the association of ideas between the visible heaven and celestial Paradise does not arise from the nature of things, but rather from ignorance and ingenuousness mixed with imagination and sentimentality; for the blue sky is a direct and therefore adequate symbol of the higher—and supra-sensory—degrees of Existence; it is indeed a distant reverberation of those degrees, and it is necessarily so since it is truly a symbol, consecrated by the sacred Scriptures and by the unanimous intuition of peoples.[6] A symbol is intrinsically so concrete and so efficacious that celestial manifestations, when they occur in our sensory world, "descend" to earth and "reascend" to Heaven; a symbolism accessible to the senses takes on the function of the supra-sensible reality which its reflects. Light-years and the relativity of the space-time relationship have absolutely nothing to do with the perfectly "exact" and "positive" symbolism of appearances and its connection at once analogical and ontological with the celestial or angelic orders. The fact that the symbol itself may be no more than an optical illusion in no way impairs its precision or its efficacy, for all appearances, including those of space and of the galaxies, are strictly speaking only illusions created by relativity.

One of the effects of modern science has been to give religion a mortal wound, by posing in concrete terms problems which only esoterism can resolve; but these problems remain unresolved, because esoterism is not listened to, and is listened to less now than ever. Faced by these new problems, religion is disarmed, and it borrows clumsily and gropingly the arguments of the enemy; it is thus compelled to falsify by imperceptible degrees its own perspective, and more and more to disavow itself. Its doctrine, it is true, is not affected, but the false opinions borrowed from its repudiators corrode it cunningly "from within"; witness, for example, modernist exegesis, the demagogic levelling down of the liturgy, the Darwinism of Teilhard de Chardin, the "worker-priests", and a "sacred art" obedient to surrealist and "abstract" influences. Scientific discoveries prove nothing to contradict the traditional positions of religion, of course, but there is no one at hand to point this out; too many "believers" consider, on the contrary, that it is time that religion "shook off the dust of the centuries", which amounts to saying, that it should "liberate" itself from its very essence and from everything which manifests that essence. The absence of metaphysical or esoteric knowledge on the one hand, and the suggestive force emanating from scientific discoveries as well as from collective psychoses on the other, make religion an almost defenceless victim, a victim that even refuses more often than not to make use of the arguments at its disposal. It would nevertheless be easy, instead of slipping into the errors of others, to demonstrate that a world fabricated by scientific influences tends everywhere to turn ends into means and means into ends, and that it results either in a mystique of envy, bitterness and hatred, or in a complacent shallow materialism destructive of qualitative distinctions. It could be demonstrated too that science, although in itself neutral—for facts are facts—is none the less a seed of corruption and annihilation in the hands of man, who in general has not enough knowledge of the underlying nature of Existence to be able to integrate—and thereby to neutralize—the facts of science in a total view of the world; that the philosophical consequences of science imply fundamental contradictions; and that man has never been so ill-known and so misinterpreted as from the moment when he was subjected to the "X-rays" of a psychology founded on postulates that are radically false and contrary to his nature.

Modern science represents itself in the world as the principal, or as the only purveyor of truth; according to this style of certainty to know Charlemagne is to know his brain-weight and how tall he was. From the point of view of total truth— let it be said once more—it is a thousand times better to believe that God created this world in six days and that the world beyond lies beneath the flat surface of the earth or in the spinning heavens, than it is to know the distance from one nebula to another without knowing that phenomena merely serve to manifest a transcendent Reality which determines us in every respect and gives to our human condition its whole meaning and its whole content. The great traditions moreover, aware that a promethean knowledge must lead to the loss of the essential and saving truth, have never prescribed nor encouraged any such accumulating of wholly external items of knowledge, for it is in fact mortal to man. It is currently asserted that such and such a scientific achievement "does honour to the human race", together with other futilities of the same kind, as if man could do honour to his nature otherwise than by surpassing himself, and as if he could surpass himself except in a consciousness of the absolute and in sanctity.

In the opinion of most men today, experimental science is justified by its results, which are in fact dazzling from a certain fragmentary point of view, but one readily loses sight not only of the decided predominance of bad results over good, but also of the spiritual devastation inherent in the scientific outlook, *a priori* and by its very nature, a devastation which its positive results—always external and partial— can never compensate. In any event, it savours of temerity in these days to dare to recall the most forgotten of Christ's sayings: "For what shall it profit a man, if he shall gain the whole world, and lose his own soul?" (Mark viii. 36.)

*   *   *

If the unbeliever recoils from the idea that all his actions will be weighed, that he will be judged and perhaps condemned by a God whom he cannot grasp, that he will have to expiate his faults or even simply his sin of indifference, it is because he has no sense of immanent equilibrium, and no sense of the majesty of Existence, and of the human state in particular. To exist is no small matter; the proof is that no man can extract from nothingness a single speck of dust; similarly, consciousness is not nothing; we cannot bestow the least spark of it on an inanimate object. The hiatus between nothingness and the least of objects is absolute, and in the last analysis this absoluteness is that of God.[7]

What is outrageous in those who assert that "God is dead"

or even "buried"[8] is that in doing so they inevitably put themselves in the place of that which they deny: whether they want to or not, they fill the vacuum left by the loss of the notion of God with psychological constructions, and this confers on them provisionally—and paradoxically—a false superiority and even a kind of pseudo-absoluteness, or a kind of false realism stamped with icy loftiness or if need be with false modesty. Thenceforth their existence—and that of the world—is terribly lonely when faced with the vacuum created by the "inexistence of God";[9] it is the world and it is themselves—they who are the brains of the world!—who henceforth carry the whole weight of universal Being instead of having the possibility of resting in it, as is demanded by human nature and above all by truth. Their poor individual existence—as distinct from Existence as such in so far as they participate in it, which moreover appears to them "absurd", if they have any idea of it at all[10]—their existence is condemned to a kind of divinity, or rather to a phantom of divinity, whence the appearance of superiority already mentioned, a posed and polished ease too often combined with a charity steeped in bitterness and in reality set against God.

The artificial isolation in question accounts moreover for the cult of "nothingness" and of "anguish", as well as for the astonishing notion of liberation by action, and even by "dedication" to action. When man is deprived of the divine "existenciation" or when he believes himself so to be, he must find something to take its place, on pain of collapsing into his own nothingness, and he does so by substituting for "existence" precisely this kind of "dedication" to action.[11] In other words, his imagination and his feelings capitulate to the ideal of the machine; for the machine has no value except by virtue of what it produces, and so man exists only by virtue of what he does, and not of what he is; but a man defined by action is no longer man, he is a beaver or an ant.

In the same line of thought, attention must be drawn to the current search for false absolutes of all planes, whence the silly theatricality of modern artists; ancient man, who had a sense of the relativity of values and who put everything in its place, appears to be mediocre by comparison, easily satisfied and hypocritical. The mystical fervour that is a part of human nature is deflected from its normal objects and squandered on absurdities; it is put into a still life or a play, when it is not applied to the trivialities which characterise the reign of the machine and of the masses.

Independently of doctrinal atheism and of cultural peculiarities, modern man moves in the world as if existence were nothing, or as if he had invented it; in his eyes it is a commonplace thing like the dust beneath his feet—more especially as he has no consciousness of the Principle at once transcendent and immanent—and he makes use of it with assurance and inadvertence in a life that has been de-consecrated into meaninglessness. Everything is conceived through the haze of a tissue of contingencies, relationships, prejudices; no phenomenon is any longer considered in itself, in its being, and grasped at its root; the contingent has usurped the rank of the absolute; man scarcely reasons any more except in terms of his imagination falsified by ideologies on the one hand and by his artificial surroundings on the other. But the eschatological doctrines, however exaggerated they may appear to the sensibilities of those whose only Gospel is their own materialism and dissipation and whose life is nothing but a flight before God, are in fact a true yardstick for man's cosmic situation; what the Revelations ask of us and what Heaven imposes or inflicts on us is what we are in reality, whether we think so or not; we know it in our heart of hearts, if only we can detach ourselves a little from the monstrous accumulation of false images entrenched in our minds. What we need is to become once again capable of grasping the value of existence and, amid the multitude of phenomena, the meaning of man; we must once again find the measure of the real! The degree of our understanding of man can be measured by our reactions to what religions teach, or to what our own religion teaches, about the hereafter.

There is something in man which can conceive the Absolute and even attain it and which, in consequence, is absolute. On this basis one can assess the extent of the aberration of those to whom it seems perfectly natural to have the right or the chance to be man, but who wish to be man without participating in the integral nature of man and the attitudes it implies. Needless to say, the possibility of denying itself, paradoxical though it appears, is also a part of human nature —for to be man is to be free in a "relatively absolute" sense —much in the same way as it is humanly possible to accept error or to throw oneself into an abyss.

It has already been pointed out that "unbelievers" no longer have the sense either of nothingness or of existence, that they no longer know the value of existence, and never look at it in relation to the nothingness from which it is miraculously detached. Miracles in the usual sense of the word are in effect only particular variants of this initial miracle —everywhere present—the miracle of the fact of existence; the miraculous and the divine are everywhere; it is the truly human outlook that is absent.

When all is said and done there are only three miracles: existence, life, intelligence; with intelligence, the curve springing from God closes on itself, like a ring which in reality has never been parted from the Infinite.

*   *   *

When the modern world is contrasted with traditional civilizations, it is not simply a question of seeking the good things and the bad things on one side or the other; good and evil are everywhere, so that it is essentially a question of knowing on which side the more important good, and on which side the lesser evil, is to be found. If someone says that such and such a good exists outside tradition, the answer is: no doubt, but one must choose the most important good, and it is necessarily represented by tradition; and if someone says that in tradition there exists such and such an evil, the answer is: no doubt, but one must choose the lesser evil, and again it is tradition that embodies it. It is illogical to prefer an evil which involves some benefits to a good which involves some evils.

Nevertheless, to confine oneself to admiring the traditional worlds is still to stop short at a fragmentary point of view, for every civilisation is a "two-edged sword"; it is a total good only by virtue of those invisible elements that determine it positively. In certain respects, every human society is bad; if its transcendent character is wholly eliminated—which amounts to dehumanizing it since an element of transcendence is essential to man though always dependent on his free consent—then the whole justification of society's existence is removed at the same time, and there remains only an ant-heap, in no way superior to any other ant-heap, since the needs of life and in consequence the right to life remain everywhere the same, whether the life be that of men or of insects. It is one of the most pernicious of errors to believe, firstly, that the human collectivity as such represents an unconditional or absolute value, and secondly that the well-being of this collectivity represents any such value or any such end in itself.

Religious civilisations, regarded as social phenomena and independently of their intrinsic value—though there is no sharp dividing line between the two—are, despite their inevitable imperfections, like sea-walls built to stem the rising tide of worldliness, of error, of subversion, of the fall and its perpetual renewal. The fall is more and more invasive, but it will be conquered in its turn by the final irruption of the divine fire, that very fire of which the religions are and always have been the earthly crystallizations. The rejection of the traditional religious frameworks on account of human abuses amounts to an assertion that the founders of religion did not know they were doing, as well as that abuses are not inherent in human nature, and that they are therefore avoidable even in societies counting millions of men, and that they are avoidable through purely human means; no more flagrant contradiction than this could well be imagined.

*   *   *

In a certain sense, Adam's sin was a sin arising from inquisitiveness, if such an expression be admissible. Originally, Adam saw contingencies in the aspect of their relationship to God and not as independent entities. Anything that is considered

43

in that relationship is beyond the reach of evil; but the desire to see contingency as it is in itself is a desire to see evil; it is also a desire to see good as something contrary to evil. As a result of this sin of inquisitiveness—Adam wanted to see the "other side" of contingency—Adam himself and the whole world fell into contingency as such; the link with the divine Source was broken and became invisible; the world became suddenly external to Adam, things became opaque and heavy, they became like unintelligible and hostile fragments. This drama is always repeating itself anew, in collective history as well as in the life of individuals.

A meaningless knowledge, a knowledge to which we have no right either by virtue of its nature, or of our capacities, and therefore by virtue of our vocation, is not a knowledge that enriches, but one that impoverishes. Adam had become poor after having acquired knowledge of contingency as such, or of contingency in so far as it limits.[12] We must distrust the fascination which an abyss can exert over us; it is in the nature of cosmic blind-alleys to seduce and to play the vampire; the current of forms does not want us to escape from its hold. Forms can be snares just as they can be symbols and keys; beauty can chain us to forms, just as it can also be a door opening towards the formless.

Or again, from a slightly different point of view: the sin of Adam consists in effect of having wished to superimpose something on existence, and existence was beatitude; Adam thereby lost this beatitude and was engulfed in the anxious and deceptive turmoil of superfluous things.[13] Instead of reposing in the immutable purity of Existence, fallen man is drawn into the dance of things that exist, and they, being accidents, are delusive and perishable. In the Christian cosmos, the Blessed Virgin is the incarnation of this snow-like purity; She is inviolable and merciful like Existence or Substance; God in assuming flesh brought with Him Existence, which is as it were His Throne; He caused it to precede Him and He came into the world by its means. God can enter the world only through virgin Existence.

*   *   *

The problem of the fall evokes the problem of the universal theophany, the problem that the world presents. The fall is only one particular link in this process; moreover it is not everywhere presented as a "shortcoming" but in certain myths it takes the form of an event unconnected with human or angelic responsibility. If there is a cosmos, a universal manifestation, there must also be a fall or falls, for to say "manifestation" is to say "other than God" and "separation".

On earth, the divine Sun is veiled; as a result the measures of things become relative, and man can take himself for what he is not, and things can appear to be what they are not; but once the veil is torn, at the time of that birth which we call death, the divine Sun appears; measures become absolute; beings and things become what they are and follow the ways of their true nature.

This does not mean that the divine measures do not reach this world, but they are as it were "filtered" by its existential shell; previously they were absolute but they become relative, hence the floating and indeterminate character of things on earth. The star which is our sun is none other than Being seen through this carapace; in our microcosm the Sun is represented by the heart.[14] It is because we live in all respects in such a carapace that we have need—that we may know who we are and whither we are going—of that cosmic cleavage which constitutes Revelation; and it could be pointed out in this connection that the Absolute never consents to become relative in a total and uninterrupted manner.

In the fall, and in its repercussions through duration, we see the element of "absoluteness" finally devoured by the element of "contingency"; it is in the nature of the sun to be devoured by the night, just as it is in the nature of light to "shine in the darkness" and not to be "comprehended". Numerous myths express this cosmic fatality, inscribed in the very nature of what could be called the "reign of the demiurge".

The prototype of the fall is in fact the process of universal manifestation. The ideas of manifestation, projection, "alienation", egress, imply those of regression, reintegration, return,

45

apocatastasis; the error of the materialists—whatever subtleties they may employ in seeking to dissolve the conventional and now "obsolete" idea of matter—is to take matter as their starting point as if it were a primordial and stable fact, whereas it is only a movement, a sort of transitory contraction of a substance that is in itself inaccessible to our senses. The matter we know, with all that it comprises, is derived from a supra-sensory and eminently plastic protomatter; it is in this protomatter that the primordial terrestrial being is reflected and "incarnated"; in Hinduism this truth is affirmed in the myth of the sacrifice of *Purusha*. Because of the tendency to segmentation inherent in this protomatter, the divine image was broken and diversified; but creatures were still, not individuals who tear one another to pieces, but contemplative states derived from angelic models and, through those models, from divine Names. It is in this sense that it could be said that in Paradise sheep lived side by side with lions; but in such a case only "hermaphrodite" prototypes—of supra-sensory spherical form—are in question, divine possibilities issuing from the qualities of "clemency" and of "rigour", of "beauty" and of "strength", of "wisdom" and of "joy". In this proto-material *hyle* occurred the creation of species and of man, a creation resembling the "sudden crystallization of a super-saturated chemical solution"[15] After the "creation of Eve"— the bipolarization of the primordial "androgyne"—there occurred the "fall", namely the "exteriorization" of the human couple, which brought in its train—since in the subtle and luminous protomatter everything was bound together and as one—the exteriorization or the "materialization" of all other earthly creatures, and thus also their "crystallization" in sensible, heavy, opaque and mortal matter.

Plato in his *Symposium* recalls the tradition that the human body, or even simply any living body, is like half a sphere; all our faculties and movements look and tend towards a lost centre—which we feel as if "in front" of us—lost, but found again symbolically and indirectly, in sexual union. But the outcome is only a grievous renewal of the drama: a fresh entry of the spirit into matter. The opposite sex is only a symbol: the true centre is hidden in ourselves, in the heart-intellect. The creature recognizes something of the lost centre in his partner; the love which results from it is like a remote shadow of the love of God, and of the intrinsic beatitude of God; it is also a shadow of the knowledge which consumes forms as by fire and which unites and delivers.

The whole cosmogonic process is found again, in static mode, in man: we are made of matter, that is to say of sensible density and of "solidification", but at the centre of our being is the suprasensible and transcendent reality, which is at once infinitely fulminating and infinitely peaceful. To believe that matter is the "alpha" which gave to everything its beginning amounts to asserting that our body is the starting point of our soul, and that therefore the origin of our *ego*, our intelligence and our thoughts is in our bones, our muscles, our organs. In reality, if God is the "omega", He is of necessity also the "alpha", on pain of absurdity. The cosmos is a "message from God to Himself by Himself" as the Sufis would say, and God is "the First and the Last", and not the Last only. There is a sort of "emanation", but it is strictly discontinuous because of the transcendence of the Principle and the essential incommensurability of the degrees of reality; emanationism, on the contrary, is based on the idea of a continuity such as would not allow the Principle to remain unaffected by manifestation. It has been said that the visible universe is an explosion and consequently a dispersion starting from a mysterious centre; what is certain is that the total Universe, the greater part of which is invisible to us in principle and not solely *de facto*, describes some such movement— in an abstract or symbolical sense—and arrives finally at the deadpoint of its expansion; this point is determined, first by relativity in general and secondly by the initial possibilities of the cycle in question. The living being itself resembles a crystallized explosion, if one can put it in that way; it is as if the being had been turned to crystal by fear in the face of God.

* * *

Man, having shut himself off from access to Heaven and

having several times repeated, within ever narrower limits, his initial fall, has ended by losing his intuition of everything that surpasses himself. He has thus sunk below his own true nature, for one cannot be fully man except by way of God, and the earth is beautiful only by virtue of its link with Heaven. Even when man retains belief, he forgets more and more what the ultimate demands of religion are; he is astonished at the calamities of this world, without its occurring to him that they may be acts of grace, since they rend, like death, the veil of earthly illusion, and thus allow man "to die before death", and so to conquer death.

Many people imagine that purgatory or hell are for those who have killed, stolen, lied, committed fornication and so on, and that it suffices to have abstained from these actions to merit Heaven. In reality, the soul is consigned to the flames for not having loved God, or for not having loved Him enough; this is understandable enough in the light of the supreme Law of the Bible: to love God with all our faculties and all our being. An absence of this love[16] does not necessarily involve murder or lying or some other transgression, but it does necessarily involve indifference;[17] and indifference, which is the most generally widespread of faults, is the very hallmark of the fall. It is possible for the indifferent[18] not to be criminals, but it is impossible for them to be saints; it is they who go in by the "wide gate" and follow the "broad way", and it is of them that the book of Revelation says "So then because thou art lukewarm, and neither cold nor hot, I will spue thee out of my mouth" (Rev. iii. 16). Indifference towards truth and towards God borders on presumption and is not free from hypocrisy; its seeming harmlessness is full of complacency and arrogance; in this state of soul, the individual is contented with himself, even if he accuses himself of minor faults and appears modest, which in fact commits him to nothing but on the contrary reinforces his illusion of being virtuous. It is this criterion of indifference that makes it possible for the "average man" to be "caught in the act", and for the most surreptitious and insidious of vices to be as it were taken by the throat, and for every man to have his poverty and distress proved to him; in short, it is indifference that is "original sin", or its most general manifestation.

Indifference is diametrically opposed to spiritual impassibility or to contempt of vanities, as well as to humility. True humility is to know that we can add nothing to God and that, even if we possessed all possible perfections and had accomplished the most extraordinary works, our disappearance would take nothing away from the Eternal.

Even believers themselves are for the most part too indifferent to feel concretely that God is not only "above" us, in "Heaven", but also "ahead" of us, at the end of the world, or even simply at the end of our own lives; that we are drawn through life by an inexorable force and that at the end of the course God awaits us; that the world will be submerged and swallowed up one day by an unimaginable irruption of the purely miraculous—unimaginable because surpassing all human experience and standards of measurement. Man cannot possibly draw on his past to bear witness to anything of the kind, any more than a may-fly can expatiate on the alternation of the seasons; the rising of the sun can in no way enter into the habitual sensations of a creature born at midnight whose life will last but a day; the sudden appearance of the orb of the sun, unforeseeable by reference to any analogous phenomenon that had occurred during the long hours of darkness, would seem like an unheard of apocalyptic prodigy. And it is thus that God will come. There will be nothing but this one advent, this one presence, and by it the world of experiences will be shattered.

*   *   *

In man stamped with the fall, not only has action priority over contemplation, but it even abolishes contemplation. Normally, the alternative ought not to be in evidence, contemplation being in its essential nature neither allied to action nor at enmity with it; but fallen man is precisely not "normal" man in the absolute sense. One could also say that in certain contexts there is harmony between contemplation and action whereas in other contexts there is opposition; but any such

49

opposition is extrinsic and quite accidental. There is harmony in the sense that in principle nothing can be opposed to contemplation—this is the initial thesis of the Bhagavad Gita—and there is opposition in so far as their respective planes differ; just as it is impossible to contemplate a nearby object and at the same time the distant landscape behind it, so too it is impossible—in this connection alone—to contemplate and to act at the same time.[19]

Fallen man is man led on by action and imprisoned by it, and that is why he is also sinful man; the moral alternative arises less from action than from the exclusivism of action, that is to say, from individualism with its illusion of being situated in a "territory" other than the "territory" of God; action becomes in a sense autonomous and totalitarian, whereas it ought to be fitted into a divine context, in a state of innocence wherein the separation of action from contemplation could not take place.

Fallen man is simultaneously squeezed and torn assunder by two pseudo-absolutes: the ponderous "I" and the dissipating "thing", the subject and the object, the *ego* and the world. As soon as he wakes up in the morning man remembers who he is; and straightway he thinks of one thing or another; between *ego* and object there is a link, which is usually action, so that a ternary is implicit in the phrase: "I—do—this" or, what amounts to the same thing: "I—want—this". *Ego*, act and thing are in effect three idols, three screens hiding the Absolute; the sage is one who puts the Absolute in the place of these three terms; it is God within him who is the transcendent and real Personality, and is hence the Principle of his "I".[20] His act is then the affirmation of God, in the widest sense, and his object is again God;[21] it is this that is realized, in the most direct way possible, by quintessential prayer[22] or concentration, which embraces, virtually or effectively, the whole life and the whole world. In a more external and more general sense, every man ought to see the three elements "subject", "act" and "object" in God, as far as he is enabled to do so through his gifts and through grace.

Fallen man is a fragmentary being, and therein lies a

danger of deviation; for to be fragmentary is, strictly speaking, to lack equilibrium. In Hindu terms, one would say that primordial man, *hamsa*, was still without caste; the *brahmana* however does not correspond exactly to the *hamsa*, he is only the uppermost fragment of the *hamsa*, otherwise he would by definition possess to the full the qualification of the warrior-king, the *kshattriya*, which is not the case; but every *Avatāra* is necessarily *hamsa*, and so is every "living liberated one", every *jīvan-mukta*.

A parenthesis may be permissible at this point. Mention has often been made elsewhere of the "naturally supernatural" transcendence of the Intellect; now one must not lose sight of the fact that this transcendence can act without impediment only on condition that it is framed by two supplementary elements, one human and the other divine, namely virtue and grace. "Virtue" in this sense is not equivalent to the natural qualities which of necessity accompany a high degree of intellectuality and contemplativity, it is a conscious and permanent striving after perfection, and perfection is essentially self-effacement, generosity and love of truth; "grace" in this sense is the divine aid which man must implore and without which he can do nothing, whatever his gifts; for a gift serves no purpose if it be not blessed by God.[23] The Intellect is infallible in itself, but this does not prevent the human receptacle from being subject to contingencies which, though they cannot modify the intrinsic nature of intelligence, can none the less be opposed to its full actualization and to the purity of its radiance.

With that in mind, let us return to the problem of action. The process of the fall, and even its results as well, are repeated on a reduced scale in every external or internal act which is contrary to the universal harmony, or to any reflection of that harmony, such as a sacred Law. The man who has sinned has, in the first place, allowed himself to be seduced, and in the second place has ceased to be what he was before; he is as it were branded by the sin, and he is so of necessity, since every act must bear its fruit; every sin is a fall, and that being so it is also "the fall". Within the general conception of "sin", distinctions must be made between a "relative" or extrinsic sin, an "absolute"[24] or intrinsic sin, and a sin of intention. Sin is "relative" when it contravenes only some specific system of morality—such as polygamy in the case of Christians or wine in the case of Muslims—but then, by the very fact of this contravention, it amounts in effect for those concerned to "absolute sin", as is proved by the sanctions for the hereafter pronounced by the respective Revelations; none the less, certain "relative sins" can become legitimate—within the very framework of the Law which they contravene —under certain special circumstances; such, for example, is the case with killing in war. Sin is "absolute" or intrinsic when it is contrary to every code of morality and is excluded in all circumstances, like blasphemy, or contempt for truth. As for the sin of intention, it is externally in conformity with a particular code or with all codes of morality, but internally opposed to the divine Nature, like hyprocrisy for example. "Sin" is thus defined as an act which, firstly, is opposed to the divine Nature in one or another of its forms or modes (the reference here is to the Divine Qualities and the intrinsic virtues which reflect them) and which, secondly, engenders in principle posthumous suffering; it does so "in principle", but not always in fact, for repentance and positive acts on the one hand and the divine Mercy on the other efface sins, or can efface them. A "code of morality" in this sense is a sacred Legislation in so far as it ordains certain actions and prohibits certain others, independently of the depth or subtlety with which a particular doctrine may define its laws in other respects. This reservation is necessary because India and the Far East have conceptions of "transgression" and "Law" more finely shaded than those of the Semitic and European west, in the sense that, broadly speaking, in the East the compensatory virtue of knowledge is taken into account; it is "the lustral water without equal", as the Hindus say; and in the sense that intention plays a much more important part than most Westerners imagine, so that it can even happen, for example, that a *guru* should ordain, provisionally and with a view to some particular operation of spiritual alchemy,[25] actions which, while damaging no one, are contrary to the Law;[26] but none the less a Legislation does comprise a code of morality, and man as such is so made that he distinguishes, rightly or wrongly, between a "good" and an "evil", that is to say his perspective is of necessity fragmentary and analytical. Moreover, the statement that certain acts are opposed to the "divine Nature" is made with the reservation that metaphysically nothing can be opposed to that Nature; Islam expresses this when it affirms that nothing can be separated from the divine Will, not even sin;[27] such ideas are not unconnected with non-Semitic perspectives, which always insist strongly on the relativity of phenomena, and on the variability of definitions to accord with different aspects of truth.

It is this essential and as it were supra-formal conception of sin which explains how in a tradition remaining "archaic" and therefore to a large extent "inarticulate", like Shinto for example, an elaborated doctrine of sin is absent; the rules of purity are the supports of a primordial synthetic virtue, superior to actions and considered as conferring on them a spiritual quality. Whereas Semitic morals start from action—outside esoterism at any rate—and seem to confine virtue to the realm of action and even to define it in terms of action, the moral code of Shinto and analogous codes[28] take an interior and global virtue as their starting-point and do not see acts as independent and self-contained crystallizations; it is only *a posteriori* and as a consequence of the "externalizing" influence of time, that the need for a more analytical code of morality could make itself felt.

Sin, as has been said, retraces the fall. But sin is not the only thing that retraces it in the realm of human attitudes and activities; there are also factors much more subtle and at the same time less serious, which intervene in a well-regulated life, and are connected with the kind of spiritual influences the Arabs call *barakah*; these factors become perhaps increasingly important as the spiritual aim becomes higher. They are connected, on the most diverse levels, with the choice of things or of situations; with the intuition of the spiritual quality of forms, gestures, morally neutral actions; their domain is connected with symbolism, aesthetics, with the significance of materials, proportions, movements, in short with everything which in a sacred art, a liturgy, a protocol, has meaning and importance. From a certain point of view, all this might seem negligible, but it is no longer at all so when one thinks of the "handling of spiritual influences"—if this expression be allowable—and when one takes account of the fact that there are forms which attract the presences of angels while there are others which repel them; in the same line of thought, one can say that, in addition to obligation, there is also a kind of courtesy towards Heaven. Things have their cosmic relationships and their perfumes, and all things ought to retain something of a recollection of Paradise; life must be lived according to the forms and rhythms of primordial inno- cence and not according to those of the fall. To act according to *barakah* is to act in conformity with a kind of "divine aesthetic"; it is an external application of the "discerning of spirits" or of the "science of humours" (*ilm el-khawātir* in Arabic) as well as also of a geometry and of a music at once sacred and universal. Everything has a meaning and every- thing signifies something; to feel this and to conform to it is to avoid many errors that reason could not by itself prevent. Sacred art, which depends on this science of *barakah*, enfolds and penetrates the whole of human existence in traditional civilizations, and even constitutes all that is understood in our days by "culture", at least so far as those civilizations are con- cerned; but without this science of "benedictions" sacred art and all the forms of courtesy would remain unintelligible and would have no sense nor value whatever.

What matters to the man who is virtually liberated from the fall is to remain in holy infancy. In a certain sense, Adam and Eve were "children" before the fall and became "adult" only through it and after it; the adult age in fact reflects the reign of the fall; old age, in which the passions are silenced, once again draws near to infancy and to Paradise, at any rate in normal spiritual conditions. The innocence and con- fidence of the very young must be combined with the detach- ment and resignation of the old; the two ages rejoin one another in contemplativity, and then in nearness to God: infancy is "still" close to Him, old age is so "already". The child can find his happiness in a flower, and so can the old man; the extremes meet, and life's spiral becomes a circle as its ends are brought together once more in the divine Mercy.

NOTES

(1) In current usage, the words "objective" and "objectivity" often carry the meaning of impartiality, but it goes without saying that in the present context they are not used in that derivative and secondary sense.

(2) A contemporary writer whose name does not come to mind has written that death is something "rather stupid", but this small impertinence is in any case a characteristic example of the mentality in question. The same outlook—or the same taste—gave rise to a remark, met with a little time ago, that a certain person had perished in an "idiotic accident". It is always nature, fate, the will of God, objective reality, which is pilloried; it is subjectivity that sets itself up as the measure of things, and what a subjectivity!

(3) That is to say if one applies the intellectual norms properly applicable in this case, since it is a question of "philosophy".

(4) This distinction is necessary to meet the objection that science operates with elements inaccessible to our senses.

(5) Not that all scientists deny these realities, but science denies them, and that is quite a different thing.

(6) The word "symbol" implies "participation" or "aspect", whatever difference of level may be involved.

(7) It should not be forgotten that God as Beyond-Being, or suprapersonal Self, is absolute in an intrinsic sense, while Being or the divine Person is absolute extrinsically, that is, in relation to His manifestation or to creatures, but not in Himself, nor with respect to the Intellect which "penetrates the depths of God".

(8) There are Catholics who do not hesitate to hold such views about the Greek Fathers and the Scholastics, doubtless in order to compensate a certain "inferiority complex".

(9) In reality God is indeed not "existent" in the sense that He cannot be brought down to the level of the existence of things. In order to make it clear that this reservation implies no kind of privation it would be better to say that God is "non-inexistent".

(10) In any case the idea is restricted to the field of perception of the world and of things, and is therefore quite indirect.

(11) It is forgotten that the sages or philosophers who have determined the intellectual life of mankind for hundreds or thousands of

years—the Prophets not being now under consideration—were in no way "dedicated to action", or rather that their "dedication" was in their work, which is fully sufficient; to think otherwise is to seek to reduce intelligence or contemplation to action, and that comes well into line with existentialism.

(12) A *hadith* says: "I seek refuge with God in the face of a science which is of no use to me", and another: "One of the claims to nobility of a Moslem rests on not paying attention to what is not his concern". Man must remain in primordial innocence, and not seek to know the universe in detail. This thirst for knowledge—as the Buddha said—holds man to the *samsāra*.

(13) Compare: "You are dominated by the desire to possess more and more". (Koran cii. 1.)

(14) And the moon is the brain, which is identified macrocosmically— if the sun is Being—with the central reflection of the Principle in manifestation, a reflection susceptible to "waxing and waning" in accordance with its contingent nature and therefore also with cyclic contingencies. These correspondences are of great complexity—a single element can take on various significations—they can therefore only be mentioned in passing. It is sufficient to add that the sun itself also of necessity represents the divine Spirit manifested, and that it is on this account that it must "wane" in setting and "wax" in rising; it gives light and heat because it is the Principle, and it sets because it is but the manifestation of the Principle; the moon from this point of view is the peripheral reflection of that manifestation. Christ is the sun, and the Church is the moon; "it is expedient for you that I go away" (John xvi. 7) but the "Son of man will come again".

(15) An expression used by Guénon in speaking of the realization of the supreme Identity". It is possible to consider deification as re- sembling—in the inverse direction—its antipodes, creation.

(16) It is not exclusively a question of a *bhakti*, of an effective and sacrificial way, but simply of the fact of preferring God to the world, whatever may be the mode of this preference; "love" in the Scriptures consequently embraces also the sapiential ways.

(17) Fénelon was right to see in indifference the gravest of the soul's ills.

(18) The *ghāfilūn* of the Koran.

(19) This is what the tragedy of Hamlet expresses: facts and actions, and the exigencies of action were inescapable, but Shakespeare's hero saw through it all, he saw only principles or ideas; he plunged into things as into a morass; their very vanity, or their unreality, prevented him from acting, dissolved his action; he had before him, not this or that evil, but evil as such, and he broke himself against the inconsistency, the absurdity, the incomprehensibility of the world. Contemplation either removes action to a distance by causing the ob-

jects of action to disappear, or it renders action perfect by making God appear in the agent. The contemplativity of Hamlet had unmasked the world, but it was not yet fixed in God; it was as it were suspended between two planes of reality. In a certain sense, the drama of Hamlet is that of the *nox profunda*: it is also perhaps, in a more outward sense, the drama of the contemplative who is forced to action, but has no vocation for it; it is in any case a drama of profundity faced with the unintelligibility of the human comedy.

(20) "The Christ in me", as St. Paul would say.

(21) This corresponds to the Sufi ternary "one who invokes, the invocation, the One who is invoked" (*dhākir, dhikr, Madhkur*).

(22) Such as the *japa* of the Hindus, the *dhikr* of the mystics of Islam, or the Jesus prayer of the Hesychasts.

(23) In certain disciplines it is the *guru* who acts on behalf of God; the result in practice is the same, if account be taken of the conditions —and the imponderables—of the spiritual climate in question.

(24) Needless to say, the word "absolute" when used in connection with sin is synonymous with "mortal", it can have no more than a purely provisional and indicative function when, as in the present case, the ground it covers falls entirely within the actual framework of contingency.

(25) Islam is not ignorant of this point of view, witness the Koranic story of the mysterious sage scandalizing his disciples by actions with a secret intention, but externally illegal.

(26) Or more precisely to the "prescriptions", such as exist in Hinduism and, in the West, especially in Judaism; there can be no question of infringements such as would seriously harm the collectivity.

(27) Christianity also admits this idea because it could not do otherwise, but puts less emphasis on it.

(28) One might well wonder whether "morality" is really the right word here, but that is a matter of terminology which is of little importance when the context admits of no misunderstanding.

CHAPTER III

DIALOGUE BETWEEN HELLENISTS AND CHRISTIANS

L IKE most inter-traditional polemics, the dialogue in which Hellenism and Christianity were in opposition was to a great extent unreal. The fact that each was right on a certain plane—or in a particular "spiritual dimension"—resulted in each emerging as victor in its own way : Christianity by imposing itself on the whole Western world, and Hellenism by surviving in the very heart of Christianity and conferring on Christian intellectuality an indelible imprint.

The misunderstandings were none the less profound, and it is not difficult to see why this was so if divergences of perspective are taken into account. From the point of view of the Hellenists the Divine Principle is at the same time one and multiple; the gods personify the Divine qualities and functions and at the same time the angelic prolongations of these qualities and functions; the idea of immanence prevails over that of transcendence, at least in exoterism. The universe is an order that is so to speak architectural, deployed from the Supreme Principle by way of intermediaries, or of hierarchies of intermediaries, down to earthly creatures; all the cosmic principles and their rays are divine, or half-divine, which amounts to saying that they are envisaged in relation to their essential and functional divinity. If God gives us life, warmth and light, He does so by way of Helios or inasmuch as He is Helios; the sun is like the hand of God, it is thus divine; and since it is so in principle, why should it not be so in its sensible manifestation? This way of looking at things is based on the essential continuity between the Cause and the effect, and not on an existential discontinuity or accidentality; the world being the necessary and strictly ordered manifestation of divinity, it is, like divinity, eternal; it is, in God's eyes, a way of deploying himself "outside himself". This eternity does not imply that the world cannot undergo eclipses, but if it inevitably does so, as all mythologies teach, it is so that it may rise again in accordance with an eternal rhythm; it cannot therefore not be. The very absoluteness of the Absolute necessitates relativity; *Māyā* is without origin, say the Vedantists. There is no "gratuitous creation", nor any creation *ex nihilo*; there is a necessary manifestation *ex divino*, and this manifestation is free within the framework of its necessity, and necessary within the framework of its liberty. The world is divine through its character as a divine manifestation, or by way of the metaphysical marvel of its existence.

There is no occasion to describe here, on account of a concern for symmetry, the Christian outlook, which is that of Semitic monotheism, and is for that reason familiar to everyone. On the other hand it seems indispensable before proceeding further to clarify the fact that the Hellenistic conception of the "divinity of the world" has nothing to do with the error of pantheism, for the cosmic manifestation of God in no way detracts from the absolute transcendence appertaining to the Principle in itself, and in no way contradicts what is metaphysically acceptable in the Semitic and Christian conception of a *creatio ex nihilo*. To believe that the world is a "part" of God and that God, by his Selfhood or by his very essence, spreads himself into the forms of the world, would be a truly "pagan" conception—such as has no doubt existed here and there, even among the men of old—, and in order to keep clear of it, one must possess a knowledge that is intrinsically what would be represented on the plane of ideas by a combination between the Hellenistic "cosmosophy" and the Judeo-Christian theology, the reciprocal relationship of these two outlooks playing the part of touchstone with respect to total truth. Metaphysically speaking, the Semitic and monotheistic "creationism", as soon as it presents itself as an absolute and exclusive truth, is nearly as false as pantheism; it is so "metaphysically" because total knowledge is in question and not the opportunity of salvation alone, and "nearly" because a half-truth which tends to safeguard the transcendence of God at the expense of the metaphysical intelligibility of the world is less erroneous than a half-truth which tends to safeguard the divine nature of the world at the expense of the intelligibility of God.

If the Christian polemists did not understand that the outlook of the Greek sages was no more than the esoteric complement of the Biblical notion of creation, the Greek polemists understood even less of the compatibility between the two outlooks. It is true that one incomprehension sometimes begets another, for it is difficult to penetrate the profound intention of a strange concept when that intention remains implicit, and when in addition it is presented as destined to replace truths that are perhaps partial, but are in any case evident to those who accept them traditionally. A partial truth may be insufficient from one point of view or another, it is none the less a truth.

*   *   *

In order properly to understand the significance of this dialogue, which in some respects was but a confrontation between two monologues, one must take account of the following: as far as the Christians were concerned there was no knowledge possible without love; that is to say that in their eyes gnosis was valid only on condition that it was included within a unifying experience; by itself, and apart from the lived spiritual reality, an intellectual knowledge of the universe had no meaning to them; but eventually the Christians had to recognize the rights of a knowledge that was theoretical, and thus conceptual and proleptic, which they did by borrowing from the Greeks certain elements of their science, not without sometimes abusing Hellenism as such, with as much ingratitude as inconsistency. If a simple and rather summary formulation be permissible, one can say that for the Greeks truth is that which is in conformity with the nature of things; for the Christians truth is that which leads to God. This Christian attitude, to the extent that it tended to be exclusive, was bound to appear to the Greeks as a "foolishness"; in the eyes of the Christians the attitude of the Greeks consisted in taking thought for an end in itself, unconnected with any personal relation to God; consequently it was a "wisdom according to the flesh", since it cannot by itself regenerate the fallen and impotent will, but on the contrary by its self-sufficiency draws men away from the thirst for God and for salvation. From the Greek point of view, things are what they are whatever we may make of them; from the Christian—to speak schematically and *a priori*—our relationship to God alone makes sense. The Christians could be reproached for an outlook that was too much concerned with the will and too self-interested, and the Greeks on the one hand for too much liveliness of thought and on the other for too rational and too human a perfectionism; it was in some respects a dispute between a love-song and a mathematical theorem. It could also be said that the Hellenists were predominantly right in principle and the Christians in fact, at least in a particular sense that can be discerned without difficulty.

As for the Christian gnostics, they necessarily admitted the doctrinal anticipations of the Divine mysteries, but on condition—it cannot be too strongly emphasized—that they remained in a quasi-organic connection with the spiritual experience of gnosis-love; to know God is to love him, or rather, since the scriptural point of departure is love : to love God perfectly is to know him. To know was indeed *a priori* to conceive of supernatural truths, but to do so while making our whole being participate in this understanding; it was thus to love the divine quintessence of all gnosis, that quintessence which is "love" because it is at once union and beatitude. The school of Alexandria was fully as Christian as that of Antioch, in the sense that it saw in the acceptance of Christ the *sine qua non* of salvation; its foundations were perfectly Pauline. In St. Paul's view a conceptual and expressible gnosis is a knowing "in part" (*ex parte*), and it shall be "done away" when "that which is perfect is come",[1] namely, the totality of gnosis which, through the very fact of its totality, is "love" (*charitas*, χάριτας), the divine prototype of human gnosis. In the case of man there is a distinction—or a complementarism—between love and knowledge, but before God their polarity is surpassed and unified. In the Christian perspective this supreme degree is called "love", but in another perspective— notably in the Vedantic—one can equally well call it "knowledge", while maintaining, not that knowledge finds its totalization or its exaltation in love, but on the contrary that love (*bhakti*), being individual, finds its sublimation in pure knowledge (*jnāna*), which is universal; this second mode of expression is directly in conformity with the sapiential perspective.

*   *   *

The Christian protest is unquestionably justified in so far as it is directed to the "humanist" side of "classical" Hellenism and to the mystical ineffectuality of philosophy as such. On the other hand, it is in no way logical to reproach the Greeks with a divinization of the cosmos on the pretext that there can be no "entry" of God into the world, while admitting that Christ, and he alone, brings about just such an entry; indeed, if Christ can bring it about, it is precisely because it is possible and because it is realized *a priori* by the cosmos itself; the "avataric" marvel of Christ retraces, or humanizes, the cosmic marvel of creation or of "emanation".

From the point of view of the Platonists—in the widest sense —the return to God is inherent in the fact of existence : our being itself offers the way of return, for that being is divine in its nature, otherwise it would be nothing; that is why we must return, passing through the strata of our ontological reality, all the way to pure Substance, which is one; it is thus that we become perfectly "ourselves". Man realizes what he knows : a full comprehension—in the light of the Absolute—of relativity dissolves it and leads back to the Absolute. Here again there is no irreducible antagonism between Greeks and Christians : if the intervention of Christ can become necessary, it is not because deliverance is something other than a return, through the strata of our own being, to our true Self, but because the function of Christ is to render such a return possible. It is made possible on two planes, the one existential and exoteric and the other intellectual and esoteric; the second plane is hidden in the first, which alone appears in the full light of day, and that is the reason why for the common run of mortals the Christian perspective is only existential and separative, not intellectual and unitive. This gives rise to another misunderstanding between Christians and Platonists : while the Platonists propound liberation by Knowledge because man is an intelligence[2] the Christians envisage in their over-all doctrine a salvation by Grace because man is an existence—as such separated from God—and a fallen and impotent will. Once again, the Greeks can be reproached for having at their command but a single way, inaccessible in fact to the majority, and for giving the impression that it is philosophy that saves, just as one can reproach the Christians for ignoring liberation by Knowledge and for assigning an absolute character to our existential and volitive reality alone and to means appropriate to that aspect of our being, or for taking into consideration our existential relativity and not our "intellectual absoluteness"; nevertheless the reproach to the Greeks cannot concern their sages, any more than the reproach to the Christians can attack their gnosis, nor in a general way their sanctity.

The possibility of our return to God—wherein are different degrees—is universal and timeless, it is inscribed in the very nature of our existence and of our intelligence; our powerlessness can only be accidental, not essential. That which is principially indispensable is an intervention of the Logos, but not in every case the intervention of a particular manifestation of the Logos, unless we belong to it by reason of our situation and by virtue of that fact it chooses us; as soon as it chooses us, it occupies the place of the Absolute as far as we are concerned, and then it "is" the Absolute. It could even be said that the imperative character that Christ assumes for Christians—or for men providentially destined for Christianity—retraces the imperative character inherent in the Logos in every spiritual way, whether of the West or of the East.

*　　*　　*

One must react against the evolutionist prejudice which makes out that the thought of the Greeks "attained" to a certain level or a certain result, that is to say, that the triad Socrates—Plato—Aristotle represents the summit of an entirely "natural" thought, a summit reached after long periods of effort and groping. The reverse is the truth, in the sense that all the said triad did was to crystallize rather imperfectly a primordial and intrinsically timeless wisdom, actually of Aryan origin and typologically close to the Celtic, Germanic, Mazdean and Brahmanic esoterisms. There is in Aristotelian rationality and even in the Socratic dialectic a sort of "humanism" more or less connected with artistic naturalism and scientific curiosity, and thus with empiricism. But this already too contingent dialectic—and let us not forget that the Socratic dialogues are tinged with spiritual "pedagogy" and have something of the provisional in them—this dialectic must not lead us into attributing a "natural" character to intellections that are "supernatural" by definition, or "naturally supernatural". On the whole, Plato expressed sacred truths in a language that had already become profane—profane because rational and discursive rather than intuitive and symbolist, or because it followed too closely the contingencies and humours of the mirror that is the mind—whereas Aristotle placed truth itself, and not merely its expression, on a profane and "humanistic" plane. The originality of Aristotle and his school resides no doubt in giving to truth a maximum of rational bases, but this cannot be done without diminishing it, and it has no purpose save where there is a withdrawal of intellectual intuition; it is a "two-edged sword" precisely because truth seems thereafter to be at the mercy of syllogisms. The question of knowing whether this constitutes a betrayal or a providential readaptation is of small importance here, and could no doubt be answered in either sense.[3] What is certain is that Aristotle's teaching, so far as its essential content is concerned, is still much too true to be understood and appreciated by the protagonists of the "dynamic" and relativist or "existentialist" thought of our epoch. This last half plebeian, half demonic kind of thought is in contradiction with itself from its very point of departure, since to say that everything is relative or "dynamic", and therefore "in movement", is to say that there exists no point of view from which that fact can be established; Aristotle had in any case fully foreseen this absurdity.

The moderns have reproached the pre-Socratic philosophers —and all the sages of the East as well—with trying to construct a picture of the universe without asking themselves whether our faculties of knowledge are at the height of such an enterprise; the reproach is perfectly vain, for the very fact that we can put such a question proves that our intelligence is in principle adequate to the needs of the case. It is not the dogmatists who are ingenuous, but the sceptics, who have not the smallest idea in the world of what is implicit in the "dogmatism" they oppose. In our days some people go so far as to make out that the goal of philosophy can only be the search for a "type of rationality" adapted to the comprehension of "human realism"; the error is the same, but it is also coarser and meaner, and more insolent as well. How is it that they cannot see that the very idea of inventing an intelligence capable of resolving such problems proves, in the first place, that this intelligence exists already—for it alone could conceive of any such idea —and shows in the second place that the goal aimed at is of an unfathomable absurdity? But the present purpose is not to prolong this subject; it is simply to call attention to the parallelism between the pre-Socratic—or more precisely the Ionian— wisdom and oriental doctrines such as the *Vaisheshika* and the *Sankhya*, and to underline, on the one hand, that in all these ancient visions of the Universe the implicit postulate is the innateness of the nature of things in the intellect[4] and not a supposition or other logical operation, and on the other hand, that this notion of innateness furnishes the very definition of that which the sceptics and empiricists think they must disdainfully characterize as "dogmatism"; in this way they demonstrate that they are ignorant, not only of the nature of intellection, but also of the nature of dogmas in the proper sense of the word. The admirable thing about the Platonists is not, to be sure, their "thought", it is the content of their thought, whether it be called "dogmatic" or otherwise.

The Sophists inaugurate the era of individualistic rationalism and of unlimited pretensions; thus they open the door to all arbitrary totalitarianisms. It is true that profane philosophy also begins with Aristotle, but in a rather different sense, since the rationality of the Stagyrite tends upwards and not downwards as does that of Protagoras and his like; in other words, if a dissolving individualism originates with the Sophists—not forgetting allied spirits such as Democritus and Epicurus—Aristotle on the other hand opens the era of a rationalism still anchored in metaphysical certitude, but none the less fragile and ambiguous in its very principle, as there has more than once been occasion to point out.

However that may be, if one wants to understand the Christian reaction, one must take account of all these aspects of the spirit of Greece, and at the same time of the Biblical, mystical and "realizational" character of Christianity. Greek thought appeared in the main as a promethean attempt to appropriate to itself the light of Heaven, rashly breaking through the stages on the way to Truth; but at the same time it was largely irresistible because of the self-evidence of its content : that being so, one must not lose sight of the fact that in the East sapiential doctrines were never presented in the form of a "literature" open to all, but that on the contrary their assimilation required a corresponding spiritual method, and this is the very thing that had disappeared and could no longer be found among the Greeks of the classical epoch.

*　　*　　*

It has been said and said again that the Hellenists and the Orientals—the "Platonic" spirits in the widest sense—have become blameworthy in "arrogantly" rejecting Christ, or that they are trying to escape from their "responsibilities"—once again and always !—as creatures towards the Creator in withdrawing into their own centre where they claim to find, in their pure being, the essence of things and the Divine Reality; they thus dilute, it seems, the quality of creature and at the same time that of Creator with a sort of pantheistic impersonalism, which amounts to saying that they destroy the relationship of "obligation" between the Creator and the creature. In reality "responsibilities" are relative as we ourselves are relative in our existential specification; they cannot be less relative —or "more absolute"—than the subject to which they are related. One who, by the grace of Heaven, succeeds in escaping from the tyranny of the ego is by that very circumstance discharged from the responsibilities which the ego implies. God shows himself as creative Person in so far as—or in relation to the fact that—we are "creature" and individual, but that particular reciprocal relationship is far from exhausting all our ontological and intellectual nature; that is to say, our nature cannot be exhaustively defined by notions of "duty", of "rights", nor by other fixations of the kind. It has been said that the "rejection" of the Christic gift on the part of the "Platonic" spirit constitutes the subtlest and most Luciferan perversity of the intelligence; this argument, born of an instinct of self-preservation, wrong in its inspiration but comprehensible on its own plane, can easily and far more pertinently be turned against those who make use of it: for, if we are to be obliged at all costs to find some mental perversion somewhere, we shall find it with those who want to substitute for the Absolute a personal and therefore relative God, and temporal phenomena for metaphysical principles, and that not in connection with a childlike faith that asks nothing of anybody, but within the framework of the most exacting erudition and the most totalitarian intellectual pretension. If there is such a thing as abuse of the intelligence, it is to be found in the substitution of the relative for the Absolute, or the accident from the Substance, on the pretext of putting the "concrete" above the "abstract";[5] it is not to be found in the rejection— in the name of transcendent and immutable principles—of a relativity presented as absoluteness.

The misunderstanding between Christians and Hellenists can for the greater part be condensed to a false alternative: in effect, the fact that God resides in our deepest "being"—or at the extreme transpersonal depth of our consciousness— and that we can in principle realize him with the help of the pure and theomorphic intellect, in no way excludes the equal and simultaneous affirmation of this immanent and impersonal

Divinity as objective and personal, nor the fact that we can do nothing without his grace, despite the essentially "divine" character of the Intellect in which we participate naturally and supernaturally.

It is perfectly true that the human individual is a concrete and definite person, and responsible before a Creator, a personal and omniscient Legislator; but it is quite as true—to say the least of it—that man is but a modality, so to speak external and coagulated, of the Divinity at once impersonal and personal, and that human intelligence is such that it can in principle be conscious of this fact and thus realise its true identity. In one sense it is evidently the fallen and sinful individuality that is "ourselves"; in another sense it is the transcendant and unalterable Self; the planes are different, there is no common measure between them.

When the religious dogmatist claims for some terrestrial fact an absolute import—and the "relatively absolute" character of the same fact is not here in question—the Platonist or the Oriental appeals to principial and timeless certitudes; in other words, when the dogmatist asserts that "this is", the gnostic immediately asks: "by virtue of what possibility?" According to the gnostic, "everything has already been"; he admits the "new" only in so far as it retraces or manifests the "ancient", or rather the timeless, uncreated "idea". The function of the celestial messages is in practice and humanly absolute, but they are not for that reason the Absolute, and as far as their form is concerned they do not pass beyond relativity. It is the same with the intellect at once "created" and "uncreated": the "uncreated" element penetrates it as light penetrates air or ether; this element is not the light, but is its vehicle, and in practice one cannot dissociate them.

There are two sources of certitude, namely, on the one hand the innateness of the Absolute in pure intelligence, and on the other the supernatural phenomenon of grace. It is amply evident—and cannot be too often repeated—that these two sources can be, and consequently must be, combined to a certain extent, but in fact the exoterists have an interest in setting them one against the other, and they do so by denying to intelligence its supernatural essence and by denying the innateness of the Absolute, as well as by denying grace to those who think differently from themselves. An irreducible opposition between intellection and grace is as artificial as it could be, for intellection is also a grace, but it is a static and innate grace; there can be absolutely no reason why this kind of grace should not be a possibility and should never be manifested, seeing that by its very nature it cannot not be. If anyone objects that in such matters grace is not in question but something else, the answer must be that in that case grace is not necessary, since there are only two alternatives: either grace is indispensable, and if so intellection is a grace, or intellection is not a grace, and if so grace is not indispensable.

If theologians admit, with the Scriptures, that one cannot enunciate an essential truth about Christ "unless by the Holy Spirit", they must also admit that one cannot enunciate an essential truth about God without the intervention of the same Spirit; the truths of the wisdom of Greece, like the metaphysical truths of all peoples, cannot therefore be robbed of their character in so far as it is both "supernatural" and in principle a means of salvation.

From a certain point of view, the Christian argument is the historicity of the Christ-Saviour, whereas the Platonic or "Aryan" argument is the nature of things or the Immutable. If, to speak symbolically, all men are in danger of drowning as a consequence of the fall of Adam, the Christian saves himself by grasping the pole held out to him by Christ, whereas the Platonist saves himself by swimming; but neither course weakens or neutralizes the effectiveness of the other. On the one hand there are certainly men who do not know how to swim or who are prevented from doing so, but on the other hand swimming is undeniably among the possibilities open to man; the whole thing is to know what counts most in any situation whether individual or collective.[6] We have seen that Hellenism, like all directly or indirectly sapiential doctrines, is founded on the axiom man—intelligence rather than man—will, and that is one of the reasons why it had to appear as inoperative in the eyes of a majority of Christians; but only of a majority because the Christian gnostics could not apply such a reproach to the Pythagoreans and Platonists; the gnostics could not do otherwise than admit the primacy of the intellect, and for that reason the idea of divine redemption meant to them something very different from and more far-reaching than a mysticism derived from history and a sacramental dogmatism. It is necessary to repeat once more—as others have said before and better—that sacred facts are true because they retrace on their own plane the nature of things, and not the other way round: the nature of things is not real or normative because it evokes certain sacred facts. The principles, essentially accessible to pure intelligence—if they were not so man would not be man, and it is almost blasphemy to deny that human intelligence considered in relation to animal intelligence has a supernatural side—the universal principles confirm the sacred facts, which in their turn reflect those principles and derive their efficacy from them; it is not history, whatever it may contain, that confirms the principles. This relationship is expressed by the Buddhists when they say that spiritual truth is situated beyond the distinction between objectivity and subjectivity, and that it derives its evidence from the depths of Being itself, or from the innateness of Truth in all that is.

In the sapiential perspective the divine redemption is always present; it pre-exists all terrestrial alchemy and is its celestial model, so that it is always thanks to this eternal redemption—whatever may be its vehicle on earth—that man is freed from the weight of his vagaries and even, *Deo volente*, from that of his separative existence; if "my Words shall not pass away" it is because they have always been. The Christ of the gnostics is he who is "before Abraham was" and from whom arise all the ancient wisdoms; a consciousness of this, far from diminishing a participation in the treasures of the historical Redemption, confers on them a compass that touches the very roots of Existence.

NOTES

(1) I Cor. xiii. 8.

(2) Islam, in conformity with its "paracletic" character, reflects this point of view—which is also that of the *Vedanta* and of all other forms of gnosis—in a Semitic and religious mode, and realizes it all the more readily in its esoterism; like the Hellenist, the Moslem asks first of all: "What must I know or admit, seeing that I have an intelligence capable of objectivity and of totality?" and not *a priori* "What must I want, since I have a will that is free, but fallen?"

(3) With Pythagoras one is still in the Aryan East; with Socrates-Plato one is no longer wholly in that East—in reality neither "Eastern" nor "Western", that distinction having no meaning for an archaic Europe—but neither is one wholly in the West; whereas with Aristotle Europe begins to become specifically "Western" in the current and cultural sense of the word. The East—or a particular East—forced an entry with Christianity, but the Aristotelian and Caesarean West finally prevailed, only to escape in the end from both Aristotle and Caesar, but by the downward path. It is opportune to observe here that all modern theological attempts to "surpass" the teaching of Aristotle can only follow the same path, in view of the falsity of their motives, whether implicit or explicit. What is really being sought is a graceful capitulation before evolutionary "scientism", before the machine, before an activist and demagogic socialism, a destructive psychologism, abstract art and surrealism, in short before modernism in all its forms—that modernism which is less and less a "humanism" since it de-humanizes, or that individualism which is ever more infra-individual. The moderns, who are neither Pythagoricians nor Vedantists, are surely the last to have any right to complain of Aristotle.

(4) In the terminology of the ancient cosmologists one must allow for its symbolism: when Thales saw in "water" the origin of all things, it is as certain as can be that Universal Substance—the Prakriti of the Hindus—is in question and not the sensible element. It is the same with the "air" of Anaximenes of Miletus, or with the "fire" of Heraclitus.

(5) It is really an abuse of language to qualify as "abstract" everything that is above the phenomenal order.

(6) In other words: if one party cannot logically deny that there are men who save themselves by swimming, no more can the other party deny that there are men who are saved only because a pole is held out to them.

CHAPTER IV

THE SHAMANISM OF THE RED INDIANS

THE word "Shamanism" is used here to include the traditions of prehistoric origin that are associated with mongoloid peoples, including the American Indians.[1] In Asia, Shamanism properly so called is met with not only in Siberia, but also in Tibet (in the form of *Bon-Po*) and in Mongolia, Manchuria and Korea. The pre-Buddhist Chinese tradition, with its Confucian and Taoist branches, is attached to the same traditional family, and the same applies to Japan, where Shamanism has given rise to the specifically Japanese *Shinto* tradition. Characteristic of all these doctrines is a complementary opposition of Heaven and Earth, and a cult of Nature, the latter being envisaged in relation to its essential causality and not to its existential accidentality; they are also distinguished by a certain parsimony in their eschatology— very apparent even in Confucianism—and above all by the central function of the Shaman, assumed in China by the *Tao-tse*[2] and in Tibet by the lamas concerned with divination and exorcism.[3] China and Japan have been mentioned, not in order that their native traditions should simply be assimilated to Siberian Shamanism, but in order to indicate the place they occupy in relation to the primitive tradition of the yellow races, a tradition of which Shamanism is the most direct and also, it must be admitted, the most uneven and the most ambiguous continuation. These last words suggest the need for some enquiry into the spiritual value of the Siberian and American forms of Shamanism. The general impression is one of the very widest differences of level, but one thing is certain, and it is that among the Red Indians, to whom attention will hereafter be confined, something primordial and pure has been preserved, despite all the obscurations that may have been superimposed in certain tribes, perhaps mostly in relatively recent times.

Documents bearing testimony to the spiritual quality of the Red Indians are numerous. A white man who was captured by them in his early infancy at the beginning of the nineteenth century, and who lived until his twentieth year among tribes who had never had the smallest contact with a missionary (Kickapoo, Kansas, Omaha, Osage) says: "It is certain however that they acknowledge, at least so far as my acquaintance extends, one supreme, all powerful and intelligent Being, viz., the Great Spirit, or the Giver of Life, who created and governs all things. They believe in general that, after the hunting grounds had been formed and supplied with game, he created the first red man and woman, who were very large in their stature, and lived to an exceeding old age; that he often held councils and smoked with them, gave them laws to be obeyed and taught them how to take game and cultivate corn: but that in consequence of their disobedience, he withdrew from and abandoned them to the vexations of the Bad Spirit, who had since been instrumental to all their degeneracy and sufferings. They believe him of too exalted a character to be directly the author of evil, and that, notwithstanding the offences of his red children, he continues to shower down on them all the blessings they enjoy; in consequence of this parental regard for them, they are truly filial and sincere in their devotions, and pray to him for such things as they need, and return thanks for such good things as they receive. . . . In all the tribes I have visited, the belief in a future state of existence, and in future rewards and punishments is prevalent. . . . This belief in their accountability to the Great Spirit makes the Indians generally scrupulous and enthusiastic observers of all their traditionary, tuitive, and exemplary dogmas; and it is a fact worthy of remark that neither frigidity, indifference, nor hypocrisy in regard to sacred things, is known to exist among them".[4]

Another testimony, deriving this time from a Christian source, runs as follows: "Belief in a supreme Being is firmly rooted in the culture of the Chippewas. This Being, called

73

Kiche Manito, or Great Spirit, was far removed from them. Prayers were rarely addressed directly to him alone and sacrifices were only offered to him at the feast of the Midewiwin initiates. My informants spoke of him in a tone of submission and extreme reverence. 'He has placed all things on earth and takes care of everything', added an old man, the most powerful medicine-man of the Short Ear Lake Reservation. One old woman of the same Reservation stated that when praying the ancient Indians first of all addressed *Kiche Manito* and afterwards the other great spirits, the *Kitchi Manito* who live in the winds, the snow, the thunder, the tempest, the trees, and in all things. One aged Shaman called Vermilion was convinced that 'all the Indians in his country knew God long before the White men came there; but they did not ask Him for particular things as they do now that they have become Christians. They expected favours from their own special protectors'. Less powerful than *Kiche Manito* were the divinities inhabiting Nature and also the guardian spirits. The belief of the Chippewas in a life after death is made plain by their burial and mourning customs; but they have a tradition that souls after death go towards the West 'where the sun sets', or 'towards the prairies where are situated the camping-grounds of blessing and eternal happiness' ".[5]

The writer's point of view not being compatible with evolutionism, to say the least of it, the reader will not find in these pages any suggestion of a belief in a crude and pluralistic origin of religions, nor any reason for casting doubt on the "monotheistic" aspect of the tradition of the Indians,[6] more especially because polytheism pure and simple is never anything but a degeneration, and therefore a relatively late phenomenon, and in any case much less widespread than is ordinarily supposed. Primordial monotheism has nothing specifically Semitic about it and is best described as a "pan-monotheism"; were it not so, polytheism could not have been derived from it. This monotheism subsists, or has left some traces, among peoples of the most diverse kind, including the Pygmies of Africa. In the Americas, the Fuegians, for instance, know but a single God dwelling beyond the stars; he has no body and does not sleep; stars are his eyes; he has always been and will never die; he has created the world and given to men rules of action. Among the Indians of North America, both those of the Plains and of the Forests, the divine Unity is no doubt less exclusively affirmed and in some cases even seems to be veiled; nevertheless among these peoples nothing is to be found strictly comparable to the anthropomorphic polytheism of the ancient Europeans. It is true that there are several "Great Powers",[7] but these Powers are either subordinated to a supreme Power which resembles *Brahma* much more nearly than Jupiter, or they are regarded as a totality or as a supernatural Substance of which we ourselves are parts, as a Sioux explained to the writer. In order to understand this last point, which would represent pantheism if it were taken as a full statement of the concept in question, one must know that ideas concerning the Great Spirit are attached either to the "discontinuous" reality of the Essence, which implies a transcendentalism,[8] or to the "continuous" reality of Substance, which implies a panentheism; nevertheless in the consciousness of the Red Indians the relation of Substance has more importance than that of Essence. One sometimes hears of a magical power animating all things, including man, called *Manito* (Algonquin) or *Orenda* (Iroquois); this power is coagulated or personified, according to the case, in things and beings, including those that belong to the invisible and animistic world; it also becomes crystallized in connection with some human subject, as a "totem" or "guardian angel" (the *orayon* of the Iroquois).[9] All this is correct, but with the reservation that the word "magic" which is sometimes used in this connection is far too limitative, and is even erroneous in the sense that it defines a cause in terms of a partial effect. However that may be, the important thing to remember is that the Red Indian theism, while it is not a pluralism of the Mediterranean and "pagan" type, is no nearer to coinciding with the Abrahamic monotheism; it is more in the nature of a somewhat "fluid" theosophy—there being no sacred Scripture—akin to Vedic and Far-Eastern conceptions. It is also important to note the emphasis on the

75

aspects of "life" and "power" in the Red Indian outlook, which is entirely characteristic of a warlike and more or less nomadic mentality.

Certain tribes, especially the Algonquins and Iroquois, make a distinction between the demiurge and the supreme Spirit; the former often assumes a rôle that borders on the burlesque, even on the luciferian. Such a conception of the creative Power, and of the primordial dispenser of the arts, is far from being confined to the Red Indians, as is proved, to choose one example only, by the mythologies of the Ancient World where the misdeeds of the Titans stand side by side with those of the gods. In Biblical terms, it can be said that there is no terrestrial Paradise without its serpent, and that without the serpent there can be no fall and therefore no human drama, nor any reconciliation with Heaven. The creation being in any case something that stands apart from God, a deifugal tendency must necessarily be inherent in it, so much so that it can be considered under two aspects, the one divine and the other demiurgic or luciferian. The Red Indians mingle these two aspects, nor are they alone in doing so: one need only recall the case of the god Susano-o, in the Japanese mythology, the turbulent genius of sea and storm. In short, the demiurge (called *Nanabozho, Mishabozho* and *Napi* by the *Algonquins,* and *Tharonhiawagon* by the Iroquois) is none other than *Māyā,* the primordial principle that combines both the creative power and the world itself, and is *natura naturans* as well as *natura naturata. Māyā* is beyond good and evil, she expresses both plenitude and privation, the divine and the all too human, and even the titanic and the demonic; sentimental moralism finds it difficult to understand an ambiguity of that order.

So far as cosmogony is concerned, the Red Indian does not really envisage a *creatio ex nihilo,* but rather a sort of transformation. In a celestial world situated above the visible sky there lived in the beginning semi-divine beings, the prototypic and normative personages whom earthly man has to imitate in all thngs. That heavenly world knew only peace; but a time came when some of these beings sowed the seeds of discord, and then occurred the great change: they were banished down to earth and became the ancestors of all earthly creatures. Some, however, were able to remain in Heaven, and these are the geniuses of every essential activity, such as hunting, war, love, cultivation. Consequently, what we call "creation" is, according to the Indians, a change of state or a descent: this view implies an "emanationist" point of view in the positive and legitimate sense of the word, and this point of view is in perfect agreement with the predominance among the Indians of the idea of Substance, that is to say of a "non-discontinuous" Reality. The image is that of a spiral or a star, and not one of concentric circles that are discontinuous in relation to the centre, although this second conception must never be lost sight of: the two images are complementary, but the accent is sometimes on the one and sometimes on the other.

What is the precise meaning in concrete terms of this Red Indian idea that everything is "animated"? It means, in principle and metaphysically, that, whatever be the object envisaged, there springs from its existential centre an ontological ray, made up of "being", "consciousness" and "life", whereby the object in question is attached, through its subtle or animistic root, to its luminous and celestial protoype; from this it follows that in principle it is possible for us to attain the heavenly Essence by taking anything whatever as starting point. Things are coagulations of universal Substance, but Substance is not affected (this is crucial) by those accidents in the slightest degree. Substance is not things, but things are it, and they are so by virtue of their existence and of their qualities; this is the inner meaning of the polysynthetic animism of the Red Indians, and it is this acute consciousness of the homogeneity of the world of phenomena that explains their spiritual naturalism, and also their refusal to detach themselves from nature and to become engaged in a civilization made up of artifices and servitudes, and carrying within itself the seeds of petrifaction as well as of corruption. In the view

77

of the Red Indian, as in that of Far-Eastern peoples, the human is within nature and not outside it.

*   *   *

The most eminent manifestations of the Great Spirit are the cardinal points together with the Zenith and Nadir, or with Heaven and Earth, and next in order are such forms as the Sun, the Morning Star, the Rock, the Eagle, the Bison. All these manifestations are within ourselves even though their roots subsist in Divinity. Although the Great Spirit is One, it comprises in itself all those qualities the traces of which we see and the effects of which we experience in the world of appearances.[10]

The East is Light and Knowledge, and also Peace; the South is Warmth and Life, therefore also Growth and Happiness; the West is fertilizing Water and also Revelation speaking in lightning and thunder; the North is Cold and Purity, or Strength. Thus it is that the Universe, at whatever level it may be considered, whether of Earth, Man or Heaven, is dependent on the four primordial determinations: Light, Heat, Water, Cold. The assigning of qualities in this way to the cardinal points is remarkable because they do not expressly symbolize either the four elements, air, fire, water, earth or their corresponding physical states, dryness, heat, moisture, cold, but rather tend to mix or combine the two sets of four unequally. Thus, North and South are respectively characterized by cold and heat but they do not represent the elements earth and fire, whereas the West corresponds at the same time both to moisture and to water. The East represents drought and above all light, but not air. This assymmetry can be explained as follows: the elements air and earth are respectively identified, in the spatial symbolism of the Universe, with Heaven and Earth, whereas fire, considered as a sacrificial and transmuting element, occupies the Centre of all things. If one takes account of the fact that Heaven synthesizes all the active aspects of both quaternaries, that of the elements (air, fire, water, earth) and that of the physical states (drought, heat, moisture, cold), and that Earth synthesizes their passive aspects, it will be seen that the symbolical definitions of the four quarters are intended as a synthesis of both poles, the one heavenly and the other earthly;[11] the North-South axis is earthly and the East-West axis is heavenly.

The factor that is common to all the Red Indians is the fourfold polarity of the cosmic qualities, but the descriptive symbolism can vary from one group to another and especially as between groups differing as much as Sioux and the Iroquois. Among the Cherokees, for instance, who belong to the latter family, East, South, West, North mean respectively success, happiness, death, adversity and are represented by the colours, red, white, black and blue; whereas among the Sioux all the cardinal points bear a positive meaning, their colour being in the same order of succession, red, yellow, black and white. However, there is evidently a relationship between North-adversity and North-purification, since trials purify and strengthen, or between West-death and West-revelation since both ideas are related to the beyond. Lastly, with the Ojibway, who belong to the Algonquin group, East is white like the light, South green like vegetation, West red or yellow like the setting sun and North black like the night. The attributions differ with the different points of view, but the fundamental symbolism with its fourfold structure and its polarities is not affected.

*   *   *

The crucial part played by the directions of space in the rite of the Calumet or Sacred Pipe is well known. This rite is the Indian's prayer, in which he speaks not only on his own behalf but also on behalf of all other creatures: the entire Universe prays together with the man who offers the Pipe to the Powers, or to *the* Power.

Mention must also be made here of the other great rites of North American Shamanism; together with that of the Pipe they make up the four principal rites, and they are the Sweat Lodge, Solitary Invocation and the Sun Dance.[12] The number four is chosen, not as marking any set limit, but because this number is sacred to the Red Indians, and also because

79

it permits a synthesis that has nothing arbitrary about it to be established.

The "Sweat Lodge" is the chief purificatory rite of the Indians; by its means man is cleansed and becomes a new being. This rite and that of the Pipe are absolutely fundamental; the one that follows is so as well, but in a rather different sense.

Solitary Invocation or "lamenting" or "sending forth a voice" is the most exalted form of prayer; it can be offered silently,[13] as circumstances dictate. It is a real spiritual retreat, through which every Indian has to pass once in his youth— but then the intention is a special one—, but he may also repeat it periodically at any time, according to his inspiration or to circumstances.

The Sun Dance is, in a sense, the prayer of the whole community; to those who take part in it this dance means, esoterically at least, their virtual union with the Solar Spirit, and thus with the Great Spirit. The Sun Dance symbolizes the attachment of the soul to God: just as the dancer is attached to the central tree by thongs that symbolize the sun's rays, so man is attached to Heaven by a mysterious bond which the Indian formerly sealed with his own blood; now he is satisfied to keep uninterrupted fast for three or four days. The dancer in this rite is like an eagle flying towards the sun: from a whistle made of eagle's bone he produces a shrill and plaintive sound while imitating the eagle's flight after a fashion, using feathers he carries in his hands. This as it were sacramental relationship with the sun leaves an ineffaceable mark on the soul.[14]

*　　*　　*

As regards the magical practices of the Shamans, one has to distinguish ordinary magic from what might be termed cosmic magic: the latter operates in virtue of the analogies between symbols and their prototypes. Everywhere in Nature, which includes man himself, one can discover possibilities of this kind; substances, forms and movements which correspond to one another qualitatively or typologically. The Shaman aims at mastering phenomena which by their nature or by accident lie outside his control by using other phenomena of an analogous (and therefore metaphysically "identical") kind which he creates himself and which are thereby brought within his own sphere of activity. The medicine-man may wish to bring rain, to stop a snow-storm, to cause the arrival of a herd of bison or to cure an illness and for this purpose he makes use of forms, colours, rhythms, incantations and wordless melodies. All this, however, would be insufficient but for the extraordinary power of concentration of the Shaman, acquired as it is through a long training carried out in solitude and silence and in contact with virgin Nature.[15] Concentration can also be the result of an exceptional gift or may come through the intervention of a celestial influence.[16]

Behind every sensible phenomenon there lies in fact a reality of an animistic order that is independent of the limitations of space and time; it is by getting into touch with these realities, or these subtle and supra-sensorial roots of things, that a Shaman is able to influence natural phenomena or to foretell the future. All this may sound strange, to say the least of it, to a modern reader whose imagination now bears different imprints and obeys different reflexes than did that of mediaeval or archaic man; his subconscious, it must be said, is warped by a mass of prejudices having intellectual or scientific pretensions. Without going into details, one need only recall, in the words of Shakespeare, that "there are more things in heaven and earth than are dreamed of in your philosophy."

But the Shamans are also, and even more particularly, expert magicians in the ordinary sense; their science works with forces of a psychic or animistic order, whether individualized or otherwise; it does not introduce, as in the case of cosmic magic, analogies between the microcosm and the macrocosm, or between the various natural reverberations of one and the same "idea". In "white magic", which is normally that of the Shamans, the forces called into play, as well as the purpose of the operation, are either beneficent or else simply neutral. In cases, however, where the spirits are mischievous and where the purpose is equally so, "black magic"

81

or sorcery is involved; when this happens, the link with the higher powers is broken, nothing is done "in God's name". It goes without saying that practices socially so dangerous or so pernicious in themselves were strictly prohibited among the Red Indians as with most other peoples;[17] this does not mean, however, that these practices did not undergo in the case of certain forest tribes, as they did in Europe at the end of the Middle Ages, something like an epidemic extension, in conformity with their sinister and contagious nature.[18]

One problem that has troubled all who take an interest in the Red Indians is that of the "Ghost Dance" which played so tragic a part in their final defeat. Contrary to current opinion, this dance was not an entirely unprecedented occurrence; several similar movements had arisen long before Wovoka, the originator of the Ghost Dance. In fact, there occurred fairly often among the tribes of the West the following phenomenon: a visionary, who is not necessarily a Shaman, undergoes an experience of death and, on coming back to life, brings a message from the beyond in the form of prophecies concerning the end of the world, the return of the dead and the creation of a new earth; there have even been references to "the rain of stars". This is followed by a call to peace and lastly by a dance designed to speed these events and protect the faithful, in this case the Indians. In a word, these messages from beyond the grave contain eschatological and "millenarist" conceptions such as are to be met with in one form or another in all mythologies and religions.[19]

The features of the Ghost Dance story which made it so special and so tragic arose out of the physical and psychological conditions prevailing at that moment. The despair of the Indians transposed these prophecies into the immediate future and conferred on them in addition a combative tone quite out of keeping with the pacific character of the original message; in any case it was not the Indians who provoked the conflict. As for the quasi-miraculous experiences of certain believers, especially among the Sioux, they seem to have been not so much phenomena of suggestion as hallucinations due to a collective psychosis and also in part to have been determined by Christian influences. Wovoka always denied having claimed to be the Christ, whereas he never denied having encountered the divine Being, which can be understood in many different ways, nor having received a message; there was, however, no reason why he should deny one thing rather than the other.[20] There seems to be no occasion to accuse Wovoka of imposture, especially as he has been described as a man of sincerity by white men who at least had no prejudice in his favour; doubtless the truth is that he too was a victim of circumstances. To see this whole movement in its proper proportions one must look at it in its traditional context, as determined by the "polyprophetism" of the Indians as well as by the apocalyptic trend common to all religions, and at the same time in its contingent and temporal context, namely, the collapse of the vital foundations of the Plains Indian civilization.

* * *

A fascinating combination of combative and stoical heroism with a priestly bearing conferred on the Indian of the Plains and Forests a sort of majesty at once aquiline and solar; hence the powerfully original and irreplaceable beauty that is associated with the red man and contributes to his prestige as a warrior and as a martyr.[21] Like the Japanese of the time of the Samurai, the Red Indian was in the deepest sense an artist in the outward manifestation of his personality: apart from the fact that his life was a ceaseless sporting with suffering and death,[22] hence also a kind of chivalrous *karma yoga*,[23] the Indian knew how to impart to this spiritual style an aesthetic adornment unsurpassable in its expressiveness.

One factor which may have caused people to regard the Red Indian as an individualist—in principle and not merely *de facto*—is the crucial importance he attaches to moral worth in men—to "character" if you will—and hence his cult of action.[24] The heroic and silent act is contrasted with the empty and prolix talking of the coward; the Indian's love of secrecy, his reluctance to express what is sacred by means of facile speeches that weaken and disperse it, can be explained in this way. The whole Red Indian character may be summed up in two words, if such a condensation be allowable : the act and the secret; the act shattering if need be, and the secret impassive. Rock-like, the Indian of former times rested in his own being, his own personality, ready to translate it into action with the impetuosity of lightning; but at the same time he remained humble before the Great Mystery, whose message, he knew, could always be discerned in the Nature around him.

Wild Nature is at one with holy poverty and also with spiritual childlikeness; she is an open book containing an inexhaustible teaching of truth and beauty. It is in the midst of his own artifices that man most easily becomes corrupted, it is they that make him covetous and impious; close to virgin Nature, who knows neither agitation nor falsehood, he had the hope of remaining contemplative like Nature herself. And it is Nature, quasi-divine in her totality, who will have the final word.

*   *   *

In order fully to understand the abruptness of the break-up of the Red Indian race one must take account of the fact that they had lived for thousands of years in a kind of paradise that was practically without limits; the Indians of the West were still living under such conditions at the beginning of the nineteenth century. Theirs was a rugged paradise, to be sure, but one that nevertheless provided an environment full of grandeur and at the same time sacred, comparable in many respects with the northern parts of Europe before the coming of the Romans.[25] The Indians identified themselves spiritually and humanly with this inviolate Nature—inviolable in their view —and accordingly they accepted all her laws, including the struggle for life, as exemplifying "the principle of the best". But as time went on, and concordantly with the development of the "Iron Age" in which passions predominate and wisdom disappears, abuses began to arise with increasing frequency; a heroic, but vindictive and cruel, individualism obscured the disinterested virtues, as indeed happened to all other warrior peoples. The privileged situation of the Indians, on the fringe of "history" and of its crushing urban civilizations, had inevitably to come to an end. There is nothing surprising in the fact that this disintegration of a paradise, which had in a certain sense grown old, coincided with modern times.[26]

Nevertheless it is abundantly clear that this account of the situation in terms of its fatality alone is one-sided and cannot extenuate or excuse the villainies of which the Indian has been a victim during several centuries. If that is not so, the concept of justice and injustice is meaningless and there have never been such things as infamy or tragedy. Apologists for the White invasion and its consequences are only too ready to argue that all peoples in all ages have committed acts of violence; violence, yes; but not necessarily acts of baseness, perpetrated, what is more, in the name of liberty, equality, fraternity, civilization, progress and "the rights of man"! The conscious, calculated, methodical, official and by no means anonymous destruction of the Red race, its traditions and culture, in North America and partly also in South America, far from having been an unavoidable process—and as such possibly excusable in the name of natural laws, provided one does not oneself claim to have outgrown those laws thanks to "civilization"—this destruction, it must be said, certainly remains one of the greatest crimes and most notable vandalisms of all human history.

That said, there remains the ineluctable aspect of things, the aspect of fatality, in virtue of which that which is possible cannot but be manifested in one way or another; however, this aspect of the world and of destiny does not prevent things from being what they are; evil remains evil at its own level. The nature of evil, and not its inevitability, constitutes its condemnation; its inevitability must be accepted, for tragedy enters perforce into the divine play, if only because the world is not God; one must not accept error, but one must be resigned to its existence. But beyond earthly destructions there is the Indestructible: "Every form you see", says Rumi, "has its archetype in the divine world, beyond space; if the form perishes what matter, since its heavenly model is indestructible? Every beautiful form you have seen, every meaningful word you have heard—be not sorrowful because all this must be lost; such is not really the case. The divine Source is immortal and its outflowing gives water without cease; since neither the one nor the other can be stopped, wherefore do you lament?. . . From the first moment when you entered this world of existence, a ladder has been set up before you. . . ."

NOTES

(1) But not the Mexicans and Peruvians, who represent later traditional filiations, such as are sometimes called "Atlantean", and who therefore no longer spring from the eyrie of the "Thunder-Bird".

(2) Not to be confused with the *Tao-shi* who are contemplative monks.

(3) The line of demarcation between *Bon-Po* and Lamaism is not always clear, each tradition having influenced the other.

(4) John D. Hunter: *Manners and Customs of Indian Tribes* (republished Minneapolis, 1957).

(5) Sister M. Inez Hilger: *Chippewa Child Life and its Cultural Background,* Washington, 1951.

(6) In 1770 a woman visionary announced to the Ogalala Sioux that the Great Spirit was angry with them; in the pictographic narratives ("winter counts") of the Ogalala, this year was given the name *Wakan Tanka Knashkiyan* ("Great Spirit in anger"). This happened at a time when the Sioux could not have come under the influence of white monotheism.

(7) The name *Wakan-Tanka*, literally "Great Sacred" (*wakan* = sacred) is commonly translated "Great Spirit" or "Great Mystery", and has also been rendered as "Great Powers", the plural being justified in view of the polysynthetic significance of the concept. It is not in any case without good reason that the Sioux have been called "the Unitarians of the American Indians".

(8) It goes without saying that this word must be understood in its proper sense, and that it has no connection with the Emersonian philosophy to which it gives a name. One might wonder, it may be said in passing, whether Emerson's works do not reveal, in addition to his German idealism, a certain influence coming from the Red Indians.

(9) This is on the whole equivalent to the *Kami* of Shintoism.

(10) Sages among the Indians are by no means ignorant of the contingent and illusory character of the cosmos: "I saw more than I can tell and I understood more than I saw; for I was seeing in a sacred manner the shapes of all things in the spirit, and the shape of all shapes as they must live together like one being". "Crazy Horse dreamed and went into the world where there is nothing but the

86

spirits of all things. That is the real world that is behind this one, and everything we see here is something like a shadow from that world." "I knew the real was yonder and the darkened dream of it was here." (Hehaka Sapa, from *"Black Elk Speaks"*, Lincoln, 1961).

(11) This means, if one considers all this symbolism in the light of alchemy, that in the polarization in question the complementary forces of the "sulphur" that "dilates" and of the "mercury" that "contracts" and "dissolves" are in equilibrium; the central fire is then equivalent to the hermetic fire at the bottom of the athanor.

(12) Other rites are more social in their scope.

(13) Cf. René Guénon: *Silence et Solitude*, in *Etudes Traditionnelles*, March, 1949.

(14) All these rites have been described by Hehaka Sapa in *The Sacred Pipe* by Joseph E. Brown: University of Oklahoma Press, 1953.

(15) A Soshoni told the writer that since the medicine-men have lived in houses they have become impure and lost much of their power.

(16) As in the case of Hehaka Sapa.

(17) Except perhaps among some very degenerate Melanesian tribes.

(18) Such practices have become rare, so the writer was told, owing to the fact that their evil consequences too often turned against the guilty, thanks to the protection enjoyed by their intended victims.

(19) Certain completely analogous movements occurred successively in Peru and in Bolivia, from the time of the Spanish conquest to the beginning of the present century.

(20) Cf. *The Ghost-Dance Religion* by James Mooney, in the *Fourteenth Annual Report of the Bureau of Ethnology to the Secretary of the Smithsonian Institution,* Washington, 1896; and also *The Prophet Dance of the North-West* by Leslie Spear in *General Series in Anthropology,* Menasha, Wisconsin, 1935.

(21) With due deference to the anti-romantic pseudo-realists who believe in nothing but the trivial. If no so-called primitive people has aroused an interest so lively and so lasting as have the Red Indians, and if they incarnate some of our nostalgias often wrongly qualified as puerile, it really must be that they are something in themselves, for 'there is no smoke without fire".

(22) A "trial by ordeal" as Hartley Burr Alexander described it.

(23) Black Elk's son told the writer that among the Indian Warriors there were some who vowed to die on the battlefield; they were called "those who do not return", and they carried special insignia, notably a staff adorned with feathers and with a recurved point. Similar information was given by the Crow Indians.

(24) "What can never be taken away from a man", one Sioux told the writer, "is his education, it can neither be removed nor can it be bought. Each man must form his own character and personality; one

who is content to slide will fall and he will carry the responsibility".
No less typical is the following thought as expressed by the same informant: "When an Indian smokes the Pipe, he directs it towards the four quarters and towards heaven and earth, and after that he must watch his tongue, his actions and his character".

(25) The Germans lived in hamlets and the Gauls in towns, but all their buildings were of wood, and this fact marks a fundamental difference between them and the Mediterranean people who lived in stone-built cities.

(26) Last Bull, formerly custodian of the sacred arrows of the Cheyennes, told the writer about an ancient prophecy of his tribe according to which a man would come from the East holding a leaf or skin covered with graphic signs; he would show this leaf and declare that it had come from the Creator of the world; and he would destroy men, trees and grasses in order to replace them with other men, other trees, other grasses.

CHAPTER V

MĀYĀ

M̄ĀYĀ is an exclusively Vedantic term, often rendered as "universal illusion", or "cosmic illusion", but she is also "divine play". She is the great theophany, the "unveiling" of God[1] "in Himself and by Himself" as the Sufis would say.[2] *Māyā* may be likened to a magic fabric woven from a warp that veils and a weft that unveils; she is a quasi-incomprehensible intermediary between the finite and the Infinite—at least from our point of view as creatures[3]—and as such she has all the multi-coloured ambiguity appropriate to her part-cosmic, part-divine nature.

The doctrine of the Vedantists is incontestably metaphysical above all others; it transmits all essential truths, although it is possible that the doctrine of the Sufis is more explicit on one point, namely, the "why" or the "how" of the projection of the "divine play". The Hindus declare without hesitation that *Māyā* is inexplicable; the Moslems for their part insist on the contrary on the "divine motivation" of the creation, in accordance with the saying: "I was a hidden treasure, I desired to be known[4] and I created the world":[5] the world is a "dimension" of the infinity of God, if the expression be allowable. In other words, if *Allāh* did not possess, among other qualities, that of "outwardness" (Az-Zāhir), He would not be God; or again, He alone has the power to introduce reality into the void.[6] It is true that opposed divine qualities—such as "outwardness" and "inwardness", "justice" and "mercy", "forgiveness" and "vengeance"[7]—are themselves already within the domain of *Māyā*, otherwise there would be no opposition between them, but each expresses none the less a mystery of the Essence or of the Supreme Self; for all divine aspects, extrinsic as well as intrinsic, are as one by virtue of the unity of the Essence.

If the world is necessary by virtue of a mystery of the divine infinity—and there must be no confusing of the perfection of necessity with constraint, nor yet of the perfection of liberty with arbitrariness—the necessity of the Creative Being arises before that of the world, and with all the more reason : what the world is to Being, Being is—*mutatis mutandis*—to the supreme Non-Being. *Māyā* includes not only the whole of manifestation, she is also affirmed already *a fortiori* "within" the Principle; the divine Principle "desiring to be known"—or "desiring to know"—stoops to the unfolding of its inward infinity, an unfolding at first potential and afterwards outward or cosmic.[8] The relationship "God-world", "Creator—creature", "Principle—manifestation", would be inconceivable if it were not prefigured in God, independently of any question of creation.

To say that *Māyā* is "inexplicable" does not mean that an insoluble problem is thereby presented; the only insoluble question is that of the "why" of the supreme Principle, of *Ātmā*, and it is insoluble because it is absurd, since the Absolute cannot be explained by anything relative; the Absolute is either incomprehensible, or of a dazzling self-evidence. On the other hand, the question of the "why" of *Māyā* is not meaningless, on condition that pure causality is in question and not some kind of anthropomorphic motivation; relativity has its sufficient reason in the Absolute, and is therefore evident by reference to the Absolute, while remaining problematic in itself. We can understand why the Absolute necessarily engenders the relative, but there is something in the relative which eludes our sense of causality, and that is the "why" of this or that chance event; we understand the theory of possibilities, but the choice, the arrangement, the coincidences of what is possible remain mysterious to us; things are obscure exactly to the extent that they belong to relativity, and if there could be such a thing as pure relativity, it would be pure obscurity and unintelligibility. But our very incomprehension is here a sort of comprehension : if we do not understand, it is because there is necessarily in the Universe a margin for the gratuitous and the inexplicable, which manifests in its way the divine liberty. Or again, if we start from the idea that the Absolute—and the Absolute alone—is perfectly intelligible and unconditionally evident, we may conclude that, correlatively, the relative is unintelligible, equivocal, doubtful; this is the point of view of the Vedantists. *Māyā* is none other than relativity, which in certain respects is more "mysterious" than the Absolute; but "mystery" then signifies something indirect, negative and chaotic. In short, the Hindus insist on this aspect of arbitrariness and indefinity precisely to the extent that they fix their gaze on the "superabundance of clarity"—as St. Thomas would say—of pure Reality.

It is from this unintelligible—and in a sense "absurd"—aspect of *Māyā* or of *Prakriti*[9] that arises in the main that disturbing element which insinuates itself into our mental crystallizations as soon as they depart from their normal function, which is indicative and not exhaustive; to speak of an absolute conformity of our thought to the Real is a contradiction in terms, since our thought is not the Real and since our sense of a partial conformity to the Real implies that our thought is separated from it or different from it. To deduce from this that total truth is inaccessible to us is an even greater error, and it is of a piece with the other, being also a product of confusion between direct knowledge and thought. The fact that we can have a perfectly adequate notion of a tree cannot possibly signify that our thought is identified with the tree, but on the other hand neither can the fact that our adequation is not an identity signify that we cannot know the tree in any way. However that may be, the desire to enclose universal Reality in an exclusive and exhaustive "explanation" brings with it a permanent disequilibrium due to the interferences of *Māyā*; moreover it is just this disequilibrium and this anxiety that are the life of modern philosophy. Nevertheless this aspect of unintelligibility, this kind of "irrationality", this elusive and almost "mocking" element in *Māyā* that condemns philosophy "according to the flesh" (St.

Paul) to a vicious circle and finally to suicide, proceeds in the last analysis from the transcendence of the Principle, which will no more allow itself to be imprisoned by blind ratiocinations than will our sensorial faculties allow themselves to be perceived by our senses; the use of the word "imprisoned" allows the "indicative" value of logical processes to remain unquestioned.

The justification for speaking of an aspect of "absurdity" in *Māyā* is that there is something inevitably contradictory in relativity, as is shown for example by the plurality of the *ego* —though it is logically unique—or by the unimaginable but undeniable limitlessness of space, of time, of number, of diversity, of matter. In comparison with the always precarious perfections of the world, the divine Person of course possesses super-eminently all the perfections the traces of which the world offers to us, but from the point of view of His super-ontological Essence, it is impossible to assert that the onto-logical restriction possesses the perfection of pure absolute-ness,[10] nor that the opposition of certain divine Names contains no kind of contradiction; none the less it is impossible to speak of "absurdity" outside manifestation, and all the more so in everything that concerns God the Creator as such and as distinguished from the supreme Divinity by the pre-sence of *Māyā*, who comes on to the stage at this point. It should be added that the opposition of the divine Names dis-appears in their ineffable origins; at the level of Being there is indeed opposition between "forgiveness" and "vengeance", but above that level these two Names are united in their common Essence; there is a "dilatation" so to speak, but not an "abolition".

"God the Creator" has just been mentioned with the addi-tion of the words "as such" : this precautionary qualification is far from being superfluous, for if one refers to "Being" one thereby implies "Non-Being" or "Super-Being", unless there is a specific intention to distinguish these terms one from an-other; in such things one must pay attention to the serious importance of shades of meaning, for one cannot speak of God in no matter what terms. When Being is distinctively defined as such, then it is not Super-Being or the supreme Self; but "God" is always "God"—where there is no express metaphysical reservation—and this means that in Him are aspects, but no compartments, and that those aspects always remain inseparable from the Divinity as a whole.

The distinction, in God, between a trans-ontological and transpersonal Essence on the one hand, and an already relative auto-determination on the other—this last is Being or the Person[11]—marks the whole difference between the strictly metaphysical or sapiential perspective on the one hand and cataphatic and ontologistic theories in so far as they are explicit on the other. Let us remember at this point that the Intellect—which is precisely what makes evident to us the absoluteness of the Self and the relativity of "objectivations"— is only "human" to the extent that it is accessible to us, but it is not so in itself; it is essentially *increatus et increabile* (Eckhart), although "accidentally" created by virtue of its reverberations in the macrocosm and in microcosms; geometrically speaking, the Intellect is a ray rather than a circle, it "emanates" from God rather than "reflecting" Him. "*Allāh* is known to Himself alone" say the Sufis; this saying, while it apparently excludes man from a direct and total knowledge, in reality enunciates the essential and mysterious divinity of pure Intellect; formulae of this kind are only fully understandable in the light of the often quoted *hadīth* : "He who knows his soul knows his Lord".

The sun, not being God, must prostrate itself every evening before the throne of *Allāh*; so it is said in Islam. Similarly *Māyā*, not being *Ātmā*,[12] can only affirm herself intermittently; the worlds spring from the divine Word and return into it. Instability is the penalty of contingency; to ask how we can know why there will be an end of the world and a resurrection amounts to asking why a respiratory phase stops at a precise moment to be followed by the opposite phase, or why a wave withdraws from the shore after submerging it, or again, why the drops from a fountain fall back to the ground. We are divine possibilities projected into the night of existence, and diversified by reason of that very projection, as water scatters into drops when it is launched into space, and also as it is crystallized when it is captured by cold.

The very notion of cosmic "manifestation"—or of "creation"—implies by way of consequence that of "reintegration". The two poles of the process of manifestation—the alpha and the omega one might say—are situated beyond matter, and to construct a science of the world on a foundation of matter, as if matter were a changeless and quasi-absolute substance testifies to a "lack of imagination" of the most disastrous kind; the new definitions of matter make no difference, since all they do is to displace the idea without surpassing its level. In reality matter passes through a cycle which our petty experience can never encompass; it is as if we noticed only the solidity of ice without knowing that ice had ever been water or that the water had ever been a cloud. In the supra-sensible protomatter, subjected to the determinations of the "Creative Breath", creatures were still "states of consciousness" turned inwards towards God and illuminated from within; through the "loss of Eden" oppositions became materialized and tainted with blood, but these conflicts of the animal and human "jungle" prove nothing against the primordial Paradise, wherein "sheep and wolves lived together in peace", for, once again, they appertain to the cosmic "exteriorization" of that "tissue of dreams" of which protomatter was made. There would be an analogous sequence of events if the conflicting notions contained in our minds were materialized, and being materialized started to tear one another to pieces. Conflicts and calamities cannot but be features of this base world—none the less so because most men need them; to seek to abolish by external means all terrestrial dissonances, instead of being resigned to a choice of the "lesser evil", results in the end in dissonances even more profound and more pernicious than before. Nothing but collective sanctity, which is possible in principle but not in fact, could transform the earth and take us out of a world of cleavages and absurdities.

Man is like a reduced image of the cosmogonic unfolding; we are made of matter, but in the centre of our being is the supra-sensible and transcendent reality, the "Kingdom of

Heaven", the "eye of the heart", the way to the Infinite. To suppose that matter—which in reality is but an instant—is "at the beginning" of the Universe, amounts to asserting that the flesh can produce intelligence, or that stone can produce flesh. If God is the "omega", He is also the "alpha" : the Word is "at the beginning" and not "at the end" alone, merely because that happens to suit the purposes of certain pseudo-religious evolutionary theories, the metaphysical nullity of which is self-evident. "Emanation" is strictly discontinuous because of the transcendence and immutability of the divine Substance, for any continuity would affect the Creator by way of the creation, *quod absit*. There is a theory—"but God knows best"—according to which the stellar universe is an immense explosion starting from an imperceptible nucleus. Whatever may be the value of this conception, the total Universe, of which the visible universe is but an insignificant cell, could be described in the same way, provided that the image is not taken literally; that is to say that the manifestation *Māyā*,[13] which in its totality clearly eludes our sensorial faculties and our imagination, describes an analogous and therefore centrifugal movement, until the possibilities lent to it by Being are exhausted. Every expansion attains sooner or later its deadpoint, its "end of the world" or its "last judgment".

Some people have arrived at the conclusion that space is spherical, but their principles and their methods cut them off from access to a truth that is none the less fundamental, without which all speculation on the destiny of the world and of things remains vain, namely, that time is no less circular, as indeed is everything that appertains to *Māyā*. A Red Indian, speaking of the "Great Spirit", very rightly called attention to the fact that "all that the Power of the World does is done in a circle. The Heavens are round . . . even the seasons form a great circle in their succession, and they always come back to their point of departure".[14] Thus it is that all that exists proceeds by way of gyratory movements, everything springs from the Absolute and returns to the Absolute;[15] it is because the relative cannot be conceived otherwise than as a "circular

95

emergence"—therefore transitory because returning to its source—from the Absolute, that space is round and that creatures encounter at the end of their lives the void from which they emerged, and then the Absolute that lent them their existence. To say that man is relative—which is a pleonasm, since he exists—amounts to saying that he will inexorably meet the Absolute; relativity is a circle, and the first of all circles; *Māyā* can be described symbolically as a great circular movement and also as a spherical state.[16] Death cannot destroy the *ego*, otherwise it would be possible to annihilate the spirit by material means, and therefore to create it by material means as well; a senseless supposition, the "less" having no absolute power—outside the quantitative domain— over the "greater". According to the degree of its conformity to its Origin, the creature will be retained or rejected by the Creator; and Existence in its totality will finally return, with Being itself, into the infinity of the Self. *Māyā* returns to *Ātmā*, although strictly speaking nothing can be taken away from *Ātmā* nor consequently return thereto.

The mission of man is to introduce the Absolute into the relative, if one may use so elliptical an expression. Herein too, by way of consequence—since man has all too often failed in his mission—lies the *rôle* of Revelation and of the *Avatāra*, as well as of miracles. In a miracle, as in other theophanies, the veil of *Māyā* is symbolically torn; miracles, Prophets, wisdom, are metaphysically necessary, it is inconceivable that they should not appear in the world of man; and man himself comprises all these aspects with respect to the terrestrial world, of which he is the centre and the opening towards Heaven, or the *pontifex*. The meaning of human life—to paraphrase a Christian formula enunciating the reciprocity between man and God—is to realize that *Ātmā* became *Māya* so that *Māyā* might become *Ātma*.[17]

NOTES

(1) In the three Semitic monotheistic religions, the name "God" necessarily embraces all that is proper to the Principle, with no re-

striction whatever, although their exoteric formulations evidently envisage the ontological aspect alone.

(2) There are various expressions of this kind. According to the *Risālat al-Ahadiyah* "He sent His ipseity by Himself from Himself to Himself...."

(3) For nothing is in reality outside the Infinite.

(4) Or "I desired to know"; that is to say, in distinctive mode and in relativity.

(5) *Hadīth qudsi.*

(6) Such a mode of expression may seem logically absurd, but its intellectual function and metaphysical scope—analogous to the no less contradictory idea of the geometrical point—will not escape those familiar with the writer's works.

(7) But not the simple or non-complementary qualities, such as "unity", "holiness", "wisdom", "beatitude". These qualities belong to the Essence, and it is our manner of dissociating them—and not their intrinsic nature—that appertains to *Māyā*. "Wisdom" is contained in "holiness" and inversely, whereas opposed qualities such as "rigour" and "clemency" are irreducible and irreversible.

(8) In Christian language—but not necessarily in theological language—one could say that the Father caused himself to be engendered as Son in order that the Son might be enabled to make himself man, or in order that God might make himself world.

(9) This does not mean that these two ideas are synonymous, but their juxtaposition signifies that *Prakriti*, the ontological "Substance", is the divine "femininity" of *Māyā*. The masculine aspect is represented by the divine Names which, in so far as they correspond to *Purusha*, determine and "fertilize" Substance, in collaboration with the three fundamental tendencies comprised in Substance (the *gunas*: *sattwa, rajas, tamas*).

(10) The adjective "pure" does not here constitute a pleonasm, given the idea of the "relatively absolute", which from the present point of view is of the highest metaphysical or even simply logical importance.

(11) One finds in the works of Meister Eckhart, Silesius, Omar Khayyam and others expressions that seem to make the "existence" of God dependent on that of man, but they really signify that the Intellect penetrates right into the "depths of God", and therefore that it can surpass the level of reality of the ontological Principle.

(12) The term *Ātmā* corresponds most nearly to "the Essence".

(13) *Māyā* non-manifested, as previously stated, is Being, *Ishwara*.

(14) Black Elk (Hehaka Sapa) in *Black Elk Speaks* (New York, 1932, reprinted University of Nebraska Press, Lincoln, U.S.A., 1961).

(15) One must always take account of the difference between the "relative Absolute" which is the Creator-Being and the "pure Ab-

solute" which is Non-Being, the Essence, the Self: the difference is exactly that between the "end of the world" and the apocatastasis, or between the *prālaya* and the *mahāprālaya*.

(16) This corresponds exactly to the Buddhist diagrams of the "round of existence" or of the "wheel of things". The *samsāra* is at the same time a circle and a rotation.

(17) It is in an analogous sense that the Buddhists say that *Shunya* (the "Void", the world) is *Nirvāna* (Extinction, the Absolute) and that *Nirvāna* is *Shunya*.

CHAPTER VI

REFLECTIONS ON NAÏVETY[1]

A NAÏVE outlook is often attributed to everyone who lived in the past. There is no simpler way of exalting oneself, and it is all the easier and more tempting because it is founded on accurate though fragmentary assessments which can be made the most of, with the help of false generalizations and arbitrary interpretations, by being related to an assumed all-embracing evolutionary progress. But the word "naïve" can be understood in more than one way, and so can other words that can be used in a more or less comparable sense. It would be better if people who use such words would first agree on what they are talking about. If to be naïve is to be direct and spontaneous, to know nothing of dissimulation and subterfuge and also no doubt nothing of certain experiences, then un-modernized peoples certainly possess—or possessed—that kind of naïvety; but if it is merely to be without intelligence or critical sense and to be open to all kinds of deception, then there is certainly no reason to suppose that our contemporaries are any less naïve than their forbears.

However that may be, there are few things that the "in-sulated" being who calls himself "modern man" endures less readily than the risk of appearing naïve; everything else can go by the board so long as the feeling of not being duped by anything is safeguarded. In reality the acme of naïvety is to believe that man can escape from naïvety on every plane, and that it is possible for him to be integrally intelligent by his own efforts; he who seeks to gain all things by cleverness ends by losing all in blindness and ineffectuality. People who reproach our ancestors for having been stupidly credulous forget in the first place that one can also be stupidly incredulous, and in the second place that the self-styled destroyers of illusion live on illusions that exemplify a credulity second to none. A simple credulity can be replaced by a complicated one, adorned with the arabesques of a studied doubt that forms part of the style, but it is still credulity; complication does not make error less false, nor stupidity less stupid.

One must get rid of the notion of hopelessly naive Middle Ages versus a breath-takingly intelligent twentieth century; against that view must be set the fact that history does not abolish simplicity of outlook, but merely displaces it, together with the fact that the most flagrant of naïveties is to fail to see naïvety where it exists. Moreover there is nothing more simplistic than a pretension to "start again from scratch" on every plane, nor than the systematic and unbelievably insolent self-uprooting characteristic of certain tendencies in the contemporary world. It is fashionable to regard, not only the people of the Middle Ages, but even those of fairly recent generations, as having been duped in every possible way, so that to resemble them would be a matter for shame; in this respect the nineteenth century seems almost as remote as the Merovingian age. Opinions now current prove that people think themselves incomparably more "realistic" than anyone has ever been, even in the recent past; what we call "our own times" or "the twentieth century" or "the atomic age" seems to hover, like an uprooted island or a fabulously "clear-headed" monad, above millennia of childishness and feckless-ness. The contemporary world is like a man ashamed of hav-ing had parents and wanting to create himself, and to re-create space, time and all physical laws as well, and seeking to extract from nothingness a world objectively perfect and sub-jectively comfortable, and all this by means of a creative activity independent of God or opposed to God. The unfort-unate thing is that attempts to create a new order of Being can only end in self-destruction.

The average young person of today tends, it seems, to hold our fathers responsible for all ills. That is a completely absurd atti-tude, for not only could our fathers reproach their fathers in the same way, and so on for ever, but also there is nothing to prove that the juniors among the youth of the present day will not one day have solid reasons to level the same reproach at their seniors. In so far as these young people make themselves out to be in principle innocent because they have no ideology and are not interested in politics, they forget that a world can go adrift precisely for that reason. A misfortune can come about because somebody does something, but it can also come about because nobody does anything, all the more so because nobody is alone in the world and other people take on the job of thinking and acting for those who do not want to do either. Modern man has collected a great mass of experiences, and is therefore rather disillusioned, but the conclusions he draws from it are so false that they virtually reduce to nothing all that has been gained, or ought to have been gained.

*   *   *

A fact that can lead to error, and one that is exploited without restraint, is the analogy between the childhood of individuals and that of peoples. The analogy is, however, only partial, and in a certain connection it is even inverse, for in that particular connection the collectivity is the opposite, or the inverted image, of the individual. In fact, whereas in individuals it is age that normally represents wisdom, in a traditional collectivity, as well as in humanity considered as a whole, wisdom coincides with the origin, that is to say, with the "apostolic period" in a civilization and with the "golden age" in humanity as a whole. On the other hand, just as every civilization declines, like the human race itself, as it gets farther from its origins and nearer to the "latter days", so does the individual decline, at any rate physically, with age; and just as the period of Revelation or the "golden age" is a time when Heaven and Earth are in contact and when angels speak with men, so the childhood of the individual is in some respects a time of innocence, of happiness and of nearness to Heaven. There is therefore a direct analogy between individual life and the cycles of the collectivity, in parallel with an inverse analogy that situates wisdom at the origin of the life of the collectivity and at the end of the life of the individual. Nevertheless, it is undeniable that an aged society has collected experiences and developed arts, though all such things be but outward manifestations, and it is precisely this fact that leads to error when the postulates of evolutionism are accepted *a priori*.

There is clearly an important distinction between a naïvety that is intrinsic and one that is extrinsic. The latter exists only accidentally and in relation to a world that is the product of certain experiences, but is also full of hypocrisy, of useless cleverness and of dissimulation. How could a man who is unaware of the existence of falsehood, or who knows it only as a deadly and exceptional sin, appear as otherwise than ingenuous to a mean-spirited and artful society? To a pathologically crafty person every normal person seems "simple"; in the eyes of a sharper it is the honest fellows who are artless. Even where a certain critical sense exists, it is far from constituting a superiority in itself, and is only an excrescence produced by an environment in which everything is falsified; it is an example of how nature produces self-defensive reflexes and adaptations that can only be explained in terms of the environment or of prevailing circumstances; there is no difficulty in admitting that the physical peculiarities of an Eskimo or a Bushman do not in themselves constitute a superiority. If the men of old sometimes appear ingenuous it is often because they are considered from the distorted point of view that is inseparable from a more or less generalized corruption; to accuse them of being childish amounts to applying a law to them retrospectively in the juridical sense. Similarly, an ancient writer may give an impression of simplicity of outlook, but if he does so, it is largely because he had not got to take account of a thousand errors still unknown nor of a thousand possibilities of misinterpretation, and also because there was no need for his dialectic to be like the Scottish dance in which the performer has to avoid breaking the eggs arranged to test his skill, seeing that the writer in question could in a large measure dispense with fine shades of meaning; words still possessed a freshness and a fulness, or a magic, which it is difficult for us to imagine, living as we do in a climate of verbal inflation.

A naïvety that is merely the accompaniment of a lack of experience is of course a purely relative affair; men in general, and collectivities in any case, cannot help being unsophisticated about experiences they have not had, or about experiences affecting possibilities they could not be expected to foresee. Those who have had such experiences have no good reason for criticizing the inexperience of others and thinking themselves superior; the worth of men is decided, not by their accumulation of experience, but by their capacity to profit from it. We may be more perspicacious than other people with respect to what we have experienced, yet at the same time more naïve than they with respect to what we have still to experience, or to what we are incapable of experiencing while others may have done so in our place; for it is one thing to have lived through an event and another to have drawn the right conclusions from it. Playing with fire because one does not know that it burns is no doubt a kind of artlessness, but jumping into a river because one has burnt a finger is certainly no better, for to be unaware that fire burns is no more artless than it is to be unaware that one can escape from fire otherwise than by drowning. The great, the classic, error is that of curing abuses by other abuses, apparently of less significance but really more fundamental because they compromise principles, or in other words, it is the error of getting rid of the disease by killing the patient.

*　　*　　*

There is a kind of naïvety with which our ancestors could be reproached on the plane of the physical sciences, which takes the form of a certain confusion between domains. For lack of experience or of observation,—although in itself that is certainly nothing to worry about,—they were sometimes inclined to overestimate the scope of cosmic correspondences. For this reason they tended unthinkingly to apply to one order laws applicable to another, and so to believe, for instance, that salamanders can resist fire, and can even put it out. They were misled by certain properties of these batrachians, and even more by a confusion between them and the "fiery spirits" of the same name; the men of old were all the more liable to such mistakes because they still knew by experience the unpredictable character of the subtle substance that envelops and penetrates the material world, or because, in other words, the barrier between the corporeal and psychic states was less solidified than in later periods. In return, the men of today are themselves more or less excusable on this same plane, but in a contrary sense, in that their total lack of experience of perceptible psychic manifestations seems to confirm them in their materialism. Nevertheless, however restricted the experience of modern man may be in things belonging to the psychic or subtle order, there are still phenomena of that kind which are in no way inaccessible to him in principle, but he treats them from the start as "superstitions" and hands them over to the occultists.

Acceptance of the psychic dimension is in any case part of religion: one cannot deny magic without straying from faith; so far as miracles are concerned, their cause surpasses the psychic plane, though their effects come by way of it. In theological language the term "superstition" tends to be confusing because it expresses two entirely different ideas, namely, on the one hand a wrong application of religious sentiment, and on the other a belief in unreal or ineffectual things. Thus spiritualism is called "superstition", but rightly so only with respect to its interpretations of phenomena and its cult, and not with respect to the phenomena themselves; on the other hand sciences like astrology are perfectly real and effectual, and imply no deviation of a pseudo-religious kind. The word "superstition" ought really not to be applied to sciences or facts that are unknown and are ridiculed although not a single word about them is understood, but to practices that are either intrinsically useless, or totally misunderstood and called upon to fill the gap left by an absence of true spirituality or of effectual rites. No less superstitious is a false or improper interpretation of a symbolism or of some coincidence, often in conjunction with fantastic fears or scruples, and so on. In these days the word "superstition" no longer means anything; when theologians use it—the point will bear repetition—one never knows whether they are finding fault with a concrete diabolism or with a mere illusion; in their eyes a magical act and a pretence at magic look like the same thing, and they do not notice the contradiction inherent in declaring in the same breath that sorcery is a great sin and that it is nothing but superstition.

But let us return to the scientific ingenuousness of the men of old. According to St. Thomas Aquinas "an error concerning the creation engenders a false science of God". This means, not that a knowledge of God demands a total knowledge of cosmic phenomena, which would anyhow be completely unrealizable, but that our knowledge must be either symbolically true or physically adequate; in the second case it must retain for us a symbolical intelligibility, for without this all science is vain and harmful. For example, human science has the right to stop short at, or to restrict itself to, the view that the earth is flat and that the heavens revolve, because the spiritual symbolism reflects adequately a real situation; but the evolutionary hypothesis is a proposition at once false and pernicious, because, apart from the fact that it is contrary to the nature of things, it takes away from man his essential significance and at the same stroke ruins the intelligibility of the world. In any human science dealing with phenomena there is always an element of error; we cannot attain to more than a relative knowledge in that domain, but it can be globally sufficient in the context of our spiritual knowledge. The ancients knew the laws of a nature that can be perceived directly, their astronomy was founded more or less on appearances, and it included errors in the material field, but not in the spiritual field since appearances are providential and carry a meaning for us, this deficiency is, however, largely compensated by the comprehensiveness of traditional knowledge, which in fact takes account of Angels, Paradises, demons, hells, and the non-evolutionary spontaneity of the creation (that is to say, the crystallization of celestial ideas in the cosmic substance), as well as of the apocalyptic end of the world, and many other conceptions as well. These conceptions, whatever the mythical form in which they may be clothed, are essential to human beings. On the other hand, a science that denies them, though it were to perform prodigies in the material observation of sensible phenomena, could never claim to conform to the principle enunciated by St. Thomas, firstly because a knowledge to essential things takes pride of place over a knowledge of secondary things, and secondly because a knowledge that excludes, both in fact and in principle, the essentials of the creation is incomparably more remote from an exact and complete adequation to truth than is a science apparently ingenuous, but whole.

If it is childish to believe, because one sees it in that way, that the earth is flat and that the sky and the stars revolve around it, it is no less childish to take the world of the senses to be the only world or the whole world, and to believe that matter, or energy if you like, is Existence as such; errors of that kind are indeed incomparably greater than that of the geocentric system. Furthermore, the materialistic and evolutionary error is, it must be insisted, immeasurably harmful, whereas a primitive and "natural" cosmology is nothing of the kind; this shows that there is no common measure at all between the insufficiency of the ancient cosmography and the global falsity—not the partial falsity—of a Promethean and Titanic science the principle of which was bequeathed to us from the decadence of Greece.

Characteristic of the ravages of "scientism" and of its special psychology is the following: if one remarks to a convinced disciple of progress that man could not possibly endure psychologically the conditions on another planet—and there is talk of colonizing other planets to relieve terrestrial over-population—he will answer without a tremor that a new kind of man with the necessary qualities will be produced. Unawareness and insensibility of this order are not far from the purely inhuman and monstrous, for to deny that which is total and inalienable in man is to scoff at the divine intention that makes us what we are, and has consecrated our nature through the "Word made flesh". Tacitus laughed at the Germans who tried to stop a torrent with their shields, but it is no less childish to believe in planetary migration, or to believe in the

establishment by purely human means of a society fully satisfied and perfectly inoffensive, and continuing to progress indefinitely. All this proves that, although man has inevitably
become less naïve in some connections, he has nevertheless
learnt nothing so far as essentials are concerned, to say the
least of it; the only thing that man left to himself is capable of
is to "... commit the oldest sins the newest kind of way".
(Shakespeare.)[2] And, the world being what it is, one is doubtless not guilty of a truism in adding that it is better to go to
heaven artlessly than to go intelligently to hell.

* * *

When one tries to reconstruct the psychology of ancestors
one nearly always makes the serious mistake of failing to take
into account the internal repercussions of corresponding external manifestations, for what matters is, not a progress towards an outward perfection, but the validity of our attitudes
towards the Unseen and the Absolute. Ways of thinking and
acting which may sometimes throw us off the track by their
appearance of ingenuousness often—and especially in the lives
of the saints—conceal an efficacy that is for that very reason
all the more profound. Despite the fact that in more recent
times man has accumulated a mass of experience and much
cleverness, he is certainly less "authentic" and less "effectual",
or less sensitive to the influx of the supernatural, than were his
remote ancestors. He may smile—for has he not at last become "civilized" and "adult"?—at some apparently artless
piece of reasoning or at an attitude that seems at first sight
childish or "pre-logical", nevertheless the potential inward
effectiveness of indications presented in that form eludes him.
It never seems to occur to historians and psychologists that the
surface components of human behaviour are always relative
and that a plus or a minus on that plane alone is never decisive, since only the internal mechanism of our contact with
higher states or with celestial prolongations is of real importance. The mental distance between a living so-called "primitive" and a "civilized" person is regarded as equivalent to
thousands of years, but experience proves that this distance,

where it exists, is equivalent to no more than a few days, for man is everywhere and always man.

*   *   *

It is not naïvety and superstition alone that change their situation, intelligence does so as well, and they all move together. One can satisfy oneself of this by reading philosophical texts or art criticisms, where an obstinate individualism tries to lift itself above the commonplace by climbing on to the stilts of a pretentious pseudo-psychology; it is as if the writers were attempting to borrow the subtlety of a Scholastic and the sensitiveness of a troubadour in order to say whether they feel hot or cold. A monstrous expenditure of mental ability is incurred in setting out opinions that have no relation to intelligence; people who are not well endowed intellectually by nature learn how to play at thinking and cannot even get on without some such imposture, while people who are well endowed are in danger of losing their power of thinking by falling in with the trend. What looks like an ascent is really a descent; ignorance and lack of intelligence are at ease in a wholly superficial refinement, and the result is a climate in which wisdom takes on an appearance of naïvety, of uncouthness and of reverie.

In our days everyone wants to appear intelligent, and would prefer to be accused of crime than of artlessness if the accompanying risks could be avoided. But since intelligence cannot be extracted from the void, subterfuges are resorted to, of which one of the most prevalent is the mania for "debunking", which enables an impression of intelligence to be conveyed at small cost, for all one need do is to assert that the normal reaction to a particular phenomenon is "prejudiced" and that it is high time it was cleared of the "legends" that surround it; if the ocean could be made out to be a pond or the Himalayas a hill, it would be done. Certain writers find it impossible to be content with establishing the fact that a particular thing or person has a particular character or destiny, as everyone had previously been content to do; they must always begin with "it has too often been said that . . ." and go on to declare that the reality is something quite different and has at last been discovered, and that up till now everyone has been "living a lie". This strategy is followed especially in dealing with evident and universally known things; it would doubtless be too simple to acknowledge in so many words that a lion is a carnivore and that he is not quite safe to meet.

However that may be, there is naïvety everywhere and there always has been, and man cannot escape from it, unless he can surpass his humanity; in this truth lie the key and the solution of the problem. For what matters is, not the question of knowing whether the dialectic or the demeanour of Plato or of anyone else are naïve or not, or whether they are so to a certain extent and no farther, (and one would like to know by what absolute standards any such question could be settled), but exclusively the fact that the sage or the saint has an inward access to concrete Truth; the most unpretentious formulation—doubtless the most "childish" in some people's eyes—can be the threshold of a Knowledge as complete and profound as knowledge can be.[3]

If the Bible is naïve, it is an honour to be naïve. If the philosophies that deny the Spirit are intelligent, there is no such thing as intelligence. A humble belief in a Paradise situated among the clouds has at least a background of inalienable Truth, but it has also and above all the background of a merciful reality in which is no deceit, and that is something beyond price.

NOTES

(1) Undesirable though it be to make frequent use of the rather awkwardly anglicized form of a French word, I follow the Oxford English Dictionary in accepting as English words by adoption the words "naïve" and "naïvety" (but not the French masculine form naïf), while retaining the diaeresis and pronouncing the word accordingly. There is in fact no good English equivalent: the words "artless", "ingenuous", "unsophisticated" and "child-like" lack the derogatory, though not unkindly, flavour of "naïve", whereas, "childish" goes too far the other way. The word "simple" is sometimes used in exactly the derogatory sense required, but this cannot be done without

risk of diluting its favourable sense, in which it denotes one of the cardinal virtues. (Translator's note).

(2) King Henry IV, part II, Act IV Scene 5.

(3) "Blessed are the poor in spirit: for their's is the kingdom of heaven" (Matt. v. 3)—"But let your communication be, Yea, yea; Nay, nay: for whatsoever is more than these cometh of evil." (Matt. v. 37)—"Except ye be converted, and become as little children, ye shall not enter into the kingdom of heaven." (Matt. xviii. 3.) "Blessed are they that have not seen, and yet have believed." (John xx. 29.)

CHAPTER VII

MAN IN THE UNIVERSE

MODERN science, which is rationalist as to its subject and materialist as to its object, can describe our situation physically and approximately, but it can tell us nothing about our extra-spatial situation in the total and real Universe. Astronomers know more or less where we are in space, in what relative "place", in which of the peripheral arms of the Milky Way, and they may perhaps know where the Milky Way is situated among the other assemblages of star-dust; but they do not know where we are in existential "space", namely, in a state of hardness and at the centre or summit thereof, and that we are simultaneously on the edge of an immense "rotation", which is not other than the current of forms, the "samsaric" flow of phenomena, the *panta rhei* of Heraclitus. Profane science, in seeking to pierce to its depths the mystery of the things that contain—space, time, matter, energy—forgets the mystery of the things that are contained : it tries to explain the quintessential properties of our bodies and the intimate functioning of our souls, but it does not know what intelligence and existence are; consequently, seeing what its "principles" are, it cannot be otherwise than ignorant of what man is.

When we look around us, what do we see? Firstly existence; secondly, differences; thirdly, movements, modifications, transformations; fourthly, disappearances. All these things together manifest a state of universal Substance : that state is at once a crystallization and a rotation, a heaviness and a dispersion, a solidification and a segmentation. Just as water is in ice, and the movement of the hub in the rim, so is God in phenomena; He is accessible in them and through them; this is the whole mystery of symbolism and of immanence. God is "the

Outward" and "the Inward", "the First" and "the Last".[1]

God is the most dazzlingly evident of all evidences. Everything has a centre; therefore the totality of things—the world —also has a centre. We are at the periphery of "something absolute", and that "something" cannot be less powerful, less conscious, less intelligent than ourselves. Men think they have "solid earth" under their feet and that they possess a real power; they feel perfectly "at home" on earth and attach much importance to themselves, whereas they know neither whence they came nor whither they are going and are drawn through life as by an invisible cord.

All things are limited. Now the idea of limitation is inseparable from that of effect, and similarly the idea of effect from that of cause; thus it is that all things, by their limitation no less than by their content, prove God, prime Cause and correspondingly limitless.

Or again : what proves the Absolute extrinsically? In the first place the relative, because it is meaningless save through the absoluteness it restricts, and in the second place the "relatively absolute", that is to say, the reflection of the Absolute in the relative. The question of intrinsic or direct proofs of the Absolute does not arise, the evidence being in the Intellect itself and consequently in all our being, so that indirect proofs can do no more than serve as supports or occasional causes; in the Intellect subject and object are not distinct, they could be said to interpenetrate. Certitude exists in fact, otherwise the word would not exist; there is therefore no reason to deny it on the plane of pure intellection and of the universal.[2]

*   *   *

The *ego* is at the same time a system of images and a cycle; it is something like a museum, and a unique and irreversible journey through that museum. The *ego* is a moving fabric made of images and tendencies; the tendencies come from our own substance, and the images are provided by the environment. We put ourselves into things, and we place things in ourselves, whereas our true being is independent of them.

Alongside this system of images and tendencies that constitutes our *ego* there are myriads of other systems of images and tendencies. Some of them are worse or less beautiful than our own, and others are better or more beautiful.

We are like foam ceaselessly renewed on the ocean of existence. But since God has put Himself into this foam, it is destined to become a sea of stars at the time of the final crystallization of spirits. The tiny system of images must become, when its terrestrial contingency is left behind, a star immortalized in the halo of Divinity. This star can be conceived on various levels; the divine Names are its archetypes; beyond the stars burns the Sun of the Self in its blazing transcendence and in its infinite peace.

Man does not choose; he follows his nature and his vocation, and it is God who chooses.

*   *   *

A man who has fallen into the mire and who knows that he can get out in this way or in that and with a certain amount of effort does not think of rebelling against natural laws nor of cursing existence; it is obvious to him that mud can exist and that there is such a thing as weight, and he only thinks of getting out of the mire. Now, we are in the mire of earthly existence and we know that we can escape from it, whatever trials we may undergo; Revelation gives us the assurance and the Intellect can become aware of the fact *a posteriori*. It is therefore absurd to deny God and to abuse the world for the sole reason that existence presents fissures which it cannot do otherwise than present, on pain of not existing and of being unable to "existentiate".

We are situated as it were under a sheet of ice which neither our five senses nor our reason enable us to pierce, but the Intellect—at once mirror of the supra-sensible and itself a supernatural ray of light—passes through it without trouble, once Revelation has allowed it to become conscious of its own nature. Religious belief also passes through this cosmic shell, in a less direct and more affective manner no doubt, but none the less intuitively in many cases; the divine Mercy, which is comprised in universal Reality and proves the fundamentally "beneficent"[3] character of that Reality, desires moreover that Revelation should intervene wherever that sheet of ice or that shell exists, so much so that we are never completely shut in, except it be in our refusal of Mercy. Mistaking the ice that imprisons us for Reality, we do not acknowledge what it shuts out and experience no desire for deliverance; we try to compel the ice to be happiness. Within the order of physical laws nobody thinks of refusing the Mercy that dwells indirectly in the nature of things : no man on the point of drowning refuses the pole held out to him; but too many men refuse Mercy in the total order, because it surpasses the narrow bounds of their daily experience and the no less narrow limits of their understanding. Man does not in general want to be saved except on condition that he need not surpass himself.

The fact that we are imprisoned in our five senses contains within itself an aspect of Mercy, paradoxical though this may appear after what has just been said. If the number of our senses were multiplied—and there is theoretically no limit in principle to their mutiplication—objective reality would tear through us like a hurricane; it would break us in pieces and crush us at the same time. Our "vital space" would be transparent, we would be as if suspended over an abyss or as if rushed through an incommensurable macrocosm, with its entrails exposed so to speak, and filled with terror. Instead of living in a maternal, charitably opaque and water-tight compartment of the universe—for the world is a matrix and death a cruel birth—we would find ourseves for ever faced with a totality of spaces or abysses, as well as with myriads of creatures and phenomena, such that no individual could possibly endure the experience. Man is made for the Absolute or the Infinite, not for limitless contingency.

Man, then, is as if buried under a sheet of ice. His experience of it takes various forms; at one time it is the cosmic ice that matter has become in its present and post-Edenic state of solidity, and at another time it is the ice of ignorance.

Goodness is in the very substance of the Universe, and for that reason it penetrates right into the matter we know, "accursed" though that matter be. The fruits of the earth and the rain from the sky, which make life possible, are nothing if not manifestations of the Goodness that penetrates everywhere and warms the world; and we carry that Goodness within ourselves, at the bottom of our chilled hearts.

*   *   *

The symbolism of a fountain reminds us that all things are by definition an exteriorization projected into a void in itself non-existent, but nevertheless perceptible in phenomena; water, in this imagery, is the "stuff that dreams are made of" (Shakespeare) which produces worlds and beings. The distance of the drops of water from their sources corresponds on the macrocosmic scale to a principle of coagulation and of hardening, also of individuation on a certain plane; the weight that makes the drops falls back is then the supernatural attraction of the divine Centre. The image of the fountain does not however take into account the degrees of reality, nor especially the absolute transcendence of the Centre or of the Principle; what is does take into account is the unity of "substance" or of "non-unreality",[4] but not the existential separation that cuts the relative off from the Absolute; the first relationship goes from the Principle to manifestation, and the second from manifestation to the Principle; that is to say, there is unicity "from the point of view" of the Principle, and diversity or separativity from the point of view of creatures in so far as they are themselves and nothing more.

In a certain sense worlds are like living bodies and beings are like the blood or like the air that courses through them; the contents as well as the containers are "illusory" projections out of the Principle,—illusory because in reality nothing can be separated from it,—but the contents are dynamic and the containers static; this distinction is not apparent in the symbolism of the fountain, but it is apparent in the symbolism of respiration or of the circulation of the blood.

The sage looks at things in connection with their necessarily imperfect and ephemeral exteriorization, but he also looks at them in connection with their perfect and eternal content. In

115

a moral and therefore strictly human and volitional context, this exteriorization coincides indirectly with the idea of "sin",[5] and that is an aspect of the matter that man, in so far as he is an active and passionate creature, must never lose sight of.

*   *   *

There has been much speculation on the question of knowing how the sage—the "gnostic"[6] or the *jnāni*—"sees" the world of phenomena, and occultists of all sorts have not refrained from putting forward the most fantastic theories on "clairvoyance" and the "third eye"; but in reality the difference between ordinary vision and that enjoyed by the sage or the gnostic is quite clearly not of the sensorial order. The sage sees things in their total context, therefore in their relativity and at the same time in their metaphysical transparency; he does not see them as if they were physically diaphanous or endowed with a mystical sonority or a visible aura, even though his vision may sometimes be described by means of such images. If we see before us a landscape and we know it to be a mirage—even if the eye alone cannot discern its true nature—we look at it otherwise than we should if it were a real landscape; a star makes a different impression on us from a firefly, even when the optical circumstances are such that the ocular sensations are the same; the sun would fill us with terror if it ceased to set.[7] In the same sort of way a spiritual vision of things is distinguished by a concrete perception of universal relationships and not by some special sensorial characteristic. The "third eye' 'is the faculty of seeing phenomena *sub specie aeternitatis* and therefore in a sort of simultaneity; to it are often added, in the nature of things, intuitions concerning modalities that are in the ordinary way imperceptible.

The sage sees causes in effects, and effects in causes; he sees God in all things, and all things in God. A science that penetrates the depths of the "infinitely great" and of the "infinitely small" on the physical plane, but denies other planes although it is they that reveal the sufficient reason of the nature we perceive and provide the key to it, such a science is a greater evil than ignorance pure and simple; it is in fact a "counter-science", and its ultimate effects cannot but be deadly. In other words, modern science is a totalitarian rationalism that eliminates both Revelation and Intellect, and at the same time a totalitarian materialism that ignores the metaphysical relativity—and therewith also the impermanence—of matter and of the world. It does not know that the supra-sensible, situated as it is beyond space and time, is the concrete principle of the world, and that it is consequently also at the origin of that contingent and changeable coagulation we call "matter".[8] A science that is called "exact"[9] is in fact an "intelligence without wisdom", just as post-scholastic philosophy is inversely a "wisdom without intelligence".

The principle of individuation produces a succession of spiritual outlooks that become ever narrower. At first, before this principle comes into play, there is the intrinsic vision of God: it consists in seeing nothing but God. The next stage in descending order is to see all things in Him; and next again, to see God in all things; in a certain sense these two kinds of seeing are equivalent or nearly so. After that comes the wholly indirect "vision" of the ordinary man: things "and" God; and finally, the ignorance that sees only things and excludes God, which amounts to saying that it reduces the Principle to manifestation or the Cause to the effect. But in reality God alone sees Himself; to see God is to see by Him.

One must know that which contains and not become dispersed among that which is contained. That which contains is in the first place the miracle of existence, and in the second place the miracle of consciousness or of intelligence, and in the third place the miracle of the joy that, like an expansive and creative power, fills as it were the existential and intellectual "spaces". All that is not capable of immortality must burn; accidents perish, Reality alone remains.

There is in every man an incorruptible star, a substance called upon to become crystallized in Immortality; it is eternally prefigured in the luminous proximity of the Self. Man disengages this star from its temporal entanglements in truth, in prayer and in virtue, and in them alone.

NOTES

(1) Koranic divine Names: *Az-Zāhir* and *Al-Bātin, Al-Awwal* and *Al-Akhir.*

(2) Modern philosophy is a liquidation of evidences, and therefore fundamentally of intelligence; it is no longer in any degree a *sophia,* but much more like a "misosophy".

(3) Although the divine nature is beyond moral specifications.

(4) That is to say, nothing can be situated outside the one Reality.

(5) "All that becomes deserves to perish" says Goethe in *Faust;* but he is mistaken in attributing the destructive function to the devil, whose rôle is in reality restricted to perversion and subversion.

(6) This word, here and elsewhere, is used in its etymological sense, and has nothing to do with anything that may historically be called "Gnosticism". It is gnosis itself that is in question and not its pseudo-religious deviations.

(7) It is not for nothing that the Vedantists describe ignorance as "mistaking a rope for a serpent".

(8) Recent interpretations may perhaps "refine" the idea of matter, but they do not rise above its level in the smallest degree.

(9) It is not really "exact", since it denies everything that it cannot prove on its own ground and by its own methods, as if the impossibility of material or mathematical proofs were a proof of non-existence.

CHAPTER VIII

THE UNIVERSALITY OF MONASTICISM AND ITS RELEVANCE IN THE MODERN WORLD

THE finding of a common denominator for phenomena as varied as the different monasticisms of the West and of the East does not appear at first sight to be an easy task, for in order to be able to define, one must have found a point of view that makes definition possible. There is however a point of view that seems to arise without difficulty out of the nature of things, granted that it is impossible to give an account of human nature otherwise than by way of its attachment, either positively or negatively, to God, for without God there is no such thing as man. From that point of view it can be said that the effort to reduce the complexity of life to a simple formula, and to a formula that is essential and liberating, arises out of whatever is most whole and most profound in the human condition, and that this same effort has led, in the most diverse spiritual climates, to the sort of institutional sanctity that constitutes monasticism.

Man was created alone and he dies alone; monasticism aspires to preserve this solitude in its metaphysically irreplaceable aspects : it aims to restore to man his primordial solitude before God, or again, it wants to bring man back to his spiritual integrity and to his totality. A perfect society would be a society of hermits, if so paradoxical a statement be admissible; nevertheless, that is exactly what the monastic community seeks to realise, for monasticism is in a certain sense an organised eremitism.

The reflections contained in the next few paragraphs may perhaps seem to some people to be truisms, but they are concerned with mental habits so ineradicable that it is difficult to underestimate their importance if one looks at the matter in the light of fundamentals. The point at issue is this : according to current opinion, monasticism is a matter of "vocation", but not in the proper sense of the word; for when a man is simple enough to take religion literally, and when he commits the indiscretion of allowing rather too spiritual opinions or attitudes to appear, people do not scruple to tell him that his place is "in a monastery", as if he were a foreign body with no right to existence outside the walls of the appropriate institution. The idea of "vocation", in itself positive, then becomes negative : the man who "receives a call" is not one who lives in the truth and is "called" because he lives in it, but one who disturbs society by causing it to become involuntarily aware of what it is. According to this more or less well-established way of looking at things, an absence of vocation —or, to put it plainly, worldliness—exists *de jure* and not merely *de facto*, and this implies that perfection exists as an optional speciality, and thus as a luxury; it is reserved for monks, and nobody thinks of wondering why it is not for everybody.

A monk will certainly never blame any man simply for living in his own age; this is self-evident, having regard to the secular clergy and lay saints; what is blameworthy is not living "in the world", but living in it badly, and thus in a certain sense creating it. When anyone reproaches a hermit or a monk for "running away from" the world, he commits a double error : firstly, he loses sight of the facts that contemplative isolation has an intrinsic value that is independent of the existence of a surrounding "world"; secondly, he pretends to forget that there are escapes that are perfectly honourable and that, if it is neither absurd nor shameful to do one's best to run away from an avalanche, it is no more so to run away from the temptations or even simply from the distractions of the world, or from our own *ego* in so far as it is rooted in this vicious circle; and let us not forget that in disencumbering ourselves of the world we disencumber the world of our own sufferings. In our days people are very ready to say that to escape from the world is to shirk "responsibilities", a completely hypocritical euphemism that dissimulates behind "altruistic" or "social" notions a spiritual laziness and a hatred of the absolute; people are happy to ignore the fact that the gift of oneself for God is always the gift of oneself for all. It is metaphysically impossible to give oneself to God in such a way that good does not ensue to the environment : to give oneself to God, though it were hidden from all men, is to give oneself to man, for this gift of self has a sacrificial value of an incalculable radiance.

From another point of view, to work for one's own salvation is like breathing, eating or sleeping; one cannot do these things for anyone else, nor yet help anyone else by abstaining from them. Egoism is taking away from others what they have need of; it is not taking for oneself something of which they know nothing or for which they have no desire.

It is not monasticism that is situated outside the world, it is the world that is situated outside monasticism. If every man lived in the love of God, the monastery would be everywhere, and it is in this sense that one can say that every saint is implicitly a monk or a hermit. Or again : just as it is possible to introduce the "world" into the framework of monasticism, since not every monk is a saint, so also it is possible to transfer monasticism, or the attitude it represents, into the world, for there can be contemplatives in any place.

*   *   *

If monasticism is defined as a "withdrawal for God", and if its universal and inter-religious character is recognised on the grounds that the thirst for the supernatural is in the nature of normal man, how can this definition be applied in the case of spiritual men who are Moslems and do not withdraw from society, or who are Buddhists and do cut themselves off but do not seem to have the idea of God? In other words, as far as Islam is concerned, how can there be a spirituality in a religion that rejects monasticism, or again, why is monasticism excluded from a religion which nevertheless possesses a mysticism, ascetic discipline and a cult of sants? To that the answer must be that one of the *raisons d'être* of Islam is precisely the possibility of a "monastery-society", if the expression be allowable : that is to say that Islam aims to carry the contemplative life into the very framework of society as a whole; it succeeds in realizing within that framework conditions of structure and of behaviour that permit of contemplative isolation in the very midst of the activities of the world. It must be added that what corresponds to the monastery for the Moslem is above all an initiatic attachment to a brotherhood and his submission—*perinde ac cadaver*—to a spiritual master, as well as the practice of supererogatory orisons, together with vigils and fasts; the isolating element with respect to the worldly is strictness in the observation of the *sunna*; the surrounding society would not think of opposing this strictness in a Moslem country, thus it takes the place in practice of the walls of a monastery. It is true that the Dervishes assemble in their *zawiyas* for their communal practices and make retreats in them lasting sometimes for several months; a few live there and consecrate their whole lives to prayer and the service of the *Shaikh*; but the result is not monasticism in a strict sense, comparable to that of Christians or Buddhists. However that may be, the famous "no monasticism in Islam" (lā rahbāniyah fī'l-islām) really means, not that contemplatives must not withdraw from the world, but on the contrary that the world must not be withdrawn from contemplatives; the intrinsic ideal of monasticism or of eremitism, namely asceticism and the mystical life, is in no way affected. And let us not forget that the "holy war" is accompanied in Islam by the same mystical justification as in Christian chivalry, notably that of the Templars; it offers a way of sacrifice and of martyrdom which united Christians and Moslems at the time of the crusades in one and the same sacrificial love of God.

In the case of Buddhism the difficulty lies in the fact that this religion, while it is essentially monastic, and is so to a degree that cannot be surpassed, seems to ignore the idea of God. Now it goes without saying that an "atheistic spirituality" is a contradiction in terms, and in fact Buddhism possesses completely the idea of a transcendent Absolute, and it possesses likewise the idea of a contact between this Absolute and man. Although Buddhism has not got the idea of a "God" in the Semitic or Aryan sense of the word, none the less it is in its own way just as conscious of the divine Reality, for it is far from neglecting the crucial ideas of absoluteness, of transcendence, of perfection, and, on the human side, of sacrifice and of sanctity; though doubtless "non-theist", it is quite certainly not "atheist". The aspect of a "personal God" appears notably in the *mahāyānic* cult of the Buddha Amitabha—the Japanese Amidism—wherein it is combined with a perspective of redemptive Mercy. Christian influences have been suggested; this is not only false, but even improbable from more than one point of view; it is forgotten that it is in accordance with the fundamental nature of things that phenomena analogous at least in their forms should occur wherever the circumstances are favourable. This prejudice concerning "influences" or "borrowings" brings to mind the ethnographer who found among the Red Indians the myth of the deluge, and ingenuously concluded that missionaries had been in touch with them; whereas this myth—or rather this recollection—is found among almost all the peoples on earth.

These last remarks afford an opportunity for a few words on the current confusion between syncretism and eclecticism, although this may perhaps carry us a little away from our subject. Syncretism is never an affair of substance : it is an assembling of heterogeneous elements into a false unity, that is to say, into a unity without real synthesis; eclecticism on the other hand is natural wherever different doctrines exist side by side, as is proved by the integration of Platonism or Aristotelianism with Christianity. The important thing in any case of the kind is that the original perspective should remain faithful to itself and should only accept alien concepts in so far as they corroborate its faithfulness by helping to illuminate the fundamental intentions of its own perspective. The Christians had no reason at all for refusing to be inspired by Greek wisdom since it was at hand, and in the same way the Moslems could not help making use to a certain extent in their mystical doctrine of Neoplatonic concepts as soon as they became aware of them; but it would be a serious mistake to speak of syncretism in these cases, on the false assumption of an analogy between them and artificial doctrines such as those of the modern Theosophical Society. There have never been borrowings between two living religions of essential elements affecting their fundamental structures, as is imagined when Amidism is attributed to the Nestorians.

As examples of Asiatic monasticisms, that of the Hindus and that of the Taoists may be mentioned, but they can scarcely be said to present difficulties comparable to those already spoken of in connection with Islam and Buddhism. Difficulties connected with religious differences are of course of very general occurrence, but that is a complex problem which the present somewhat synthetic view of monasticism as a pheno-menon of humanity need not take into account.

*   *   *

A world is absurd exactly to the extent that the contempla-tive, the hermit, the monk appear in it as a paradox or as an "anachronism". The monk however is in the present precisely because he is timeless: we live in an epoch of idolatry of the "age"; the monk incarnates all that is changeless, not through sclerosis or through inertia, but through transcendence.

This leads to certain considerations that may seem to diverge from our subject, but they bring negatively into relief the burning actuality of the monastic ideal, or simply of the religious ideal, which in the last analysis amounts to the same thing. In this world of absurd relativism in which we live, anyone who says "our times" thinks he has said all that is necessary; to identify phenomena of any kind with "other times", or still more with "times gone by", is to liquidate them; consider the hypocritical sadism concealed by words like "gone by", "out-dated" or "irreversible", which replace thought by a sort of imaginative suggestion, a "music of pre-judice" one might say. If it is found, for example, that some liturgical or ceremonial procedure offends the scientific or demagogic tastes of our age, people are relieved when they recall that the usage in question dates from the Middle Ages, or perhaps that it is "Byzantine", because they can then conclude without further ado that it has no longer any right to existence; they forget completely that there is only one question that must always be asked, namely, *why* the Byzantines did such a thing; more often than not one finds that the answer to this *why* is situated outside time, and that the reason for the existence of such a usage arises out of timeless factors. The identification of oneself with this "age", thereby removing from things all, or nearly all, intrinsic worth, is quite a new attitude, and it is arbitrarily projected into what we call retrospectively "the past". In reality our ancestors did not live in a "time", speaking subjectively and intellectually, but in a "space", that is to say, in a world of stable values wherein the flux of duration was only so to speak accidental; they had a marvellous sense of the absolute in things, and of the rooting of things in the Absolute.

Our age tends more and more to cut man off from his roots; but in seeking to "start again from scratch" and to reduce man to the purely human it succeeds only in dehumanizing him, which proves that the "purely human" is but a fiction; man is fully man only in rising above himself, and he can only do so through religion. Monasticism is there to remind us that man exists only by virtue of his permanent consciousness of the Absolute and of absolute values, and that the works of man are nothing in themselves. The desert Fathers, or Cassian, or St. Benedict, or their like, have shown that before acting one must be, and that actions are precious to the extent that the love of God animates them or is reflected in them, and tolerable to the extent that they are not opposed to that love. The fulness of being, which depends on the spirit, can in principle dispense with action; action does not carry its end in itself; Martha is certainly not superior to Mary. Man is distinguished from the animals in two essential respects, firstly by his intelligence that can reach the absolute and is consequently capable of objectivity and of a sense of the relative, and secondly by his free will, capable of choosing God and attaching itself to him; the rest is but contingency, and this is notably true of that profane and quantitative "culture" totally unknown to the primitive Church and now made into a pillar of human value, in defiance of current experience and of the evidence.

In our age man is defined, not by reference to his specific nature—which cannot be defined otherwise than in a divine context—but by reference to the inextricable consequences of a Prometheanism that has become secular : it is the works of man, or even the remote consequences of these works, which in the minds of our contemporaries determine and define man. We live in a scene-shifter's world wherein it has become almost impossible to get into touch with the primordial realities of things; at every step the prejudices and reflexes inseparable from an irreversible glissade intervene; it is as if before the Renaissance, or before the Encyclopaedists, man had not been wholly man, or as if, in order to be man, it were necessary to have passed by way of Descartes, Voltaire, Rousseau, Kant, Marx, Darwin and Freud, not forgetting—most recent of all—the inevitable Teilhard de Chardin. It is sad to see how religious convictions are all too often enveloped in an irreligious sensibility, or how such convictions are accompanied by reflexes directly opposed to them. Religious apologetics tend more and more to take their stand on the wrong ground, on which their victory is anyhow impossible, and to adopt a language that rings falsely and can convince nobody, discounting an occasional propagandist success which in no way serves religion as such; when apologetics rub shoulders with demagogy they enter upon the road to suicide. Instead of keeping to the pure and simple truth—a truth that quite obviously cannot please everyone—apologists allow themselves to be fascinated by the postulates of the adversary, as well as by his self-assurance, his dynamism, his easy success and his effective vulgarity. On the pretext of not wanting to "keep the religious message to oneself" it is extrinsically and imperceptibly "falsified", but belief in the existence of such a danger and the mention of such a word are carefully avoided; the very most that is admitted is a danger of "attenuating the message", a euphemism of which the bias is evident.

"Have dominion over the earth" says the Bible, and the partisans of progress do not miss the chance of exploiting that command to justify the ever more totalitarian industrialism of our age and to extol a "spirituality" that conforms to it. In reality it is a very long time since man has obeyed that injunction of the Creator; in order to grasp its true intention and its limits one must remember the divine command to "take no thought for the morrow" and other similar injunctions.[1] It is pure hypocrisy to make much of the Biblical sentence first quoted without situating it in its full context, for according to that style of logic it would be right to attribute an equal and absolute force to the words "be fruitful and multiply"[2] and to abolish all chastity in Christianity, and even to return to the polygamy of the Hebrews. This strange eagerness to follow the "commandments of God" might well lead, or so it seems, to many scriptural discoveries besides that of the passage that concerns agriculture, fishing, hunting and stock-rearing, and to many spiritual concerns other than the industrialization of religion.[3]

*　　*　　*

Inferiority complexes and mimetic reflexes are bad counsellors : how often does one meet with absurd reproaches levelled not only at the religion of the Middle Ages but also at that of the nineteenth century which at least was still not "atomic", as if all men who lived before ourselves had been struck with an inexplicable blindness, and as if it had been necessary to await the advent of such and such an atheistic philosopher to discover the light of a new knowledge both decisive and mysteriously unknown to all the saints. It is too readily forgotten that, if human nature has a right to its weaknesses today, which nobody disputes, it had the same right to them in the past; "progress" is most often but a transference, the exchange of one evil for another, otherwise our age would be perfect and sanctified. In the world of man, as it is in itself, it is scarcely possible to choose a good; one is always reduced to the choice of a lesser evil, and in order to determine which evil is the less, there is no alternative but to relate the question to a hierarchy of values derived from eternal realities, and that is exactly what "our age" never does.

In the Middle Ages one started from the idea that man is bad because he is a sinner, whereas in our century man is good because sin does not exist, so much so that evil is first and foremost whatever makes us believe in sin; modern humanitarianism, convinced that man is good, purports to protect man: but from whom? From man evidently, but from what man? And if evil does not come from man, from whom does it come, given the conviction that nothing intelligent exists outside the human being nor more particularly above him?

There is the prejudice of science and the prejudice of society; monasticism insists on the "one thing needful" and practices a collective pauperism free from all envy and perfectly concrete as far as individuals are concerned though the monastery itself be rich; it thus offers in its own way the answer to these two stumbling-blocks. What is a science that takes account neither of the transcendent and conscious Infinite, nor of the hereafter, nor of basic phenomena such as Revelation, miracle, pure intellection, contemplation, sanctity; and what is a social equilibrium that abolishes all real superiority and takes no account of the intrinsic nature of man nor of his ultimate destiny? The Biblical account of the creation raises a smile, but nobody understands the Semitic symbolism, which furnishes the key to things apparently naïve; it is claimed that the Church has always been "on the side of the rich", and it is forgotten that from the point of view of religion there is only man, be he rich or poor, man made up of flesh and of spirit, always exposed to suffering and dedicated to death; and if the Church as a terrestrial institution has been forced to lean on the powerful who protected her—or were supposed to protect her—she has never refused herself to the poor, and she compensates to a great extent her accidental and human imperfections by her spiritual gifts and her numberless saints, not forgetting the permanent spiritual presence which is precisely what monasticism actualizes. The Catholic Church has been reproached for its "self-sufficiency": now the Church has a thousand reasons for being "self-sufficient", since she is what she is, and offers what she offers; it is not for her to be uneasy, nor to produce her own "self-criticism", nor to "go off on a new tack", as she is expected to do by those who have no sense of her dignity. The Church has the right to repose in herself; her front-line troops are the saints; she has no need of busy demagogues who make play with "drama" and "death-throes". The saints suffice her, and she has always had them.

The success of atheistic materialism can be explained in part by the fact that it represents an extreme position; that kind of extremism fits easily into the framework of a tottering world, and is well adapted to the psychological elements to which it appeals. Christianity also represents an extreme position, but, instead of the fact being given its full value, it is dissembled—this at least is the tendency that seems to prevail —and the Christian position is adapted to that of the adversary, whereas it is precisely the extremism of the Christian message, if it is affirmed without disguise, but also without any forced "dynamism", that has the gift of fascinating and convincing. A conscious or unconscious capitulation before the arguments of the adversary evidently originates in a desire to give him the impression that the Christian absolute realizes the same kind of perfection as the progressive and socialist absolute, and any of the aspects, however essential, of the Christian absolute are disowned if they cut across the adverse tendencies, in such a way that nothing is left wherewith to oppose those tendencies except a half-absolute devoid of all originality; for there are two false attitudes : to say that one has never had anything in view but social progress, which is a ridiculous falsehood wholly unrelated to the Christian perspective, or to accuse oneself—promising the whole to do better in future—of having neglected social progress, and that is purely and simply a betrayal. What ought to be done is to put each thing in its place and to insist at every turn on what, from the religious point of view, man, life, the world and society are. Christianity is an eschatological perspective, it envisages things in relation to the hereafter or it does not envisage them at all; to pretend to adopt some other way of looking at things, or to adopt it in fact, while remaining within religion is an incomprehensible and disastrous inconsistency.

The relevance of monasticism is that it incarnates, whether one likes it or not, precisely that very thing in religion that is extreme and absolute and is of a spiritual and contemplative essence; terrestrial charity has no meaning save in connection with celestial charity. "Seek ye first the kingdom of God, and His righteousness . . ."

It is evident and inevitable that religion can and sometimes must adapt itself to changed circumstances; but care must be taken not to decide *a priori* in favour of circumstances, and not to look on them as norms just because they exist and because they please a majority. In proceeding to an adaptation it is important to adhere strictly to the religious perspective and to the hierarchy of values it implies; the inspiration must come from a metaphysical and spiritual body of criteria, and one must not give way to pressures nor especially allow any contamination by a false evaluation of things. Do we not hear of a "religion orientated towards social needs", which is either a pleonasm or else an absurdity, and even of a "spirituality of economic development" which, apart from its monstrosity, is a contradiction in terms? According to that way of thinking, error or sin need no longer be subordinated to the imperatives of truth and of spirituality, but on the contrary it is truth and spirituality that must be adapted to error and to sin; it is the opinion of the adversary that is the criterion of truth and falsehood, of good and evil.

*   *   *

But let us return for a moment to the modern scientific outlook, since it plays so decisive a part in the modern mentality. There seems to be absolutely no reason for going into raptures about space-flights; the saints in their ecstasies climb infinitely higher, and these words are used in no allegorical sense, but in a perfectly concrete sense that could be called "scientific" or "exact". In vain does modern science explore the infinitely distant and the infinitely small; it can reach in its own way the world of galaxies and that of molecules, but it is unaware —since it believes neither in Revelation nor in pure intellection—of all the immaterial and supra-sensorial worlds that as it were envelop our sensorial dimensions, and in relation to which these dimensions are no more than a sort of fragile coagulation, destined to disappear when its time comes before the blinding power of the Divine Reality. To postulate a science without metaphysic is a flagrant contradiction, for without metaphysic there can be no standards and no criteria, no intelligence able to penetrate, contemplate and co-ordinate. Both a relativistic psychologism which ignores the absolute, and also evolutionism which is absurd because contradictory (since the greater cannot come from the less) can be explained only by this exclusion of what is essential and total in intelligence.

In former days it was the object that was sometimes questioned, including the object that can be found within ourselves —an "object" being anything of which the subject can be distinctively and separatively conscious, even if it be a moral defect in the subject—but in our days there is no fear of the contradiction inherent in questioning the subject, the knower, in its intrinsic and irreplaceable aspect; intelligence as such is called in question, it is even "examined", without wondering "who" examines it—is there not talk about producing a more perfect man?—and without seeing that philosophic doubt is itself included in that same devaluation, that it falls if intelligence falls, and that at the same stroke all science and all philosophy collapse. For if our intelligence is by definition ineffectual, if we are irresponsible beings or lumps of earth, there is no sense in philosophizing.

What we are being pressed to admit is that our spirit is relative in its very essence, that this essence comprises no stable standards of measurement—as if the sufficient reason of the human intellect were not precisely that it should comprise some such standards!—and that consequently the ideas of truth and falsehood are intrinsically relative, and so always floating; and because certain consequences of accumulated errors fall foul of our innate standards and are unmasked and stigmatized by them, we are told that it is a question of habit and that we must change our nature, that is to say, that we must create a new intelligence that finds beautiful what is ugly and accepts as true what is false. The devil is essentially incapable of recognising that he is wrong, unless an admission to that effect is in his interest; so it is error become habitual that must be right at all costs, even at the cost of our intelligence and, in the last analysis, of our existence; as for the nature of things and our faculty of equating ourselves thereto, ideas of that sort are all "prejudice".

It has been said and said again that monasticism in all its forms, whether Christian or Buddhist, is a manifestation of "pessimism"; in this way the intellectual and realistic aspect of the question is evaded either through opportunism or through stupidity, and objective authentications, metaphysical ideas and logical conclusions are reduced to purely sentimental attitudes. A man who knows that an avalanche is an avalanche is accused of "pessimism"; an "optimist" is one who prefers to think that it is a patch of mist; to think serenely of death while despising distractions is to see the world painted in dark colours, but to think of death with repugnance, or to avoid thinking of it at all, while finding all the happiness of which one is capable in transitory things, that, it seems, is "courage", and shows a "sense of responsibility". It has never been easy to understand why those who put their hope in God, while possessing enough discernment to be able to read the "signs of the times", are accused of bitterness, whereas others are credited with strong and happy natures because they mistake mirages for realities. It is almost incredible that this false optimism, which is totally opposed to the Scriptures on the one hand and to the most tangible of criteria on the other, should win over men who profess to believe in God and in the future life.

*   *   *

An attempt must now be made to describe in a certain way—though there would be a thousand other ways of doing so—how the man who has attached himself to God is spiritually situated in existence, or how he takes his stand in face of the dizzy abyss that the world is. The condition of the monk—for it is he in whom interest is centred here, though the same considerations could be applied to contemplatives in general—the condition of the monk constitutes a victory over space and time, or over the world and life, in the sense that the monk situates himself by his attitude at the centre and in the present: at the centre in relation to a life full of phenomena, and in the present in relation to a life full of events. Concentration of prayer and rhythm of prayer: these are in a certain sense the two dimensions of spiritual existence in general and of monastic existence in particular. The monk withdraws from the world, he fixes himself in a definite place, and the place is central because it is consecrated to God, morally he shuts his eyes and remains where he is awaiting death, like a statue stood in a niche, as St. Francis de Sales says; by this "concentration" the monk places himself under the divine axis, he already partakes of Heaven by attaching himself concretely to God. In so doing the contemplative also withdraws from duration, for through prayer—that permanent actualization of a consciousness of the Absolute—he situates himself in a timeless instant: prayer, or the remembrance of God, is now and always, it is "always now" and already belongs to Eternity. The life of the monk, by the elimination of disordered movements, is a rhythm; now rhythm is the fixation of an instant—or of the present—in duration, in the same way as immobility is the fixation of a point—or of the centre—in space; this symbolism, founded as it is on the law of analogy, becomes concrete by virtue of a consecration to God. Thus it is that the monk holds the world in his hands and that he dominates life as well: for there is nothing precious in the world which we do not possess in this very place, if this point where we are belongs to God and if, being here for God, we belong to him; and in the same way, all our life is in that instant in which we choose God and not vanities.

In the temporal dimension that stretches ahead of us there are only three certitudes: that of death, that of Judgment and that of the Eternal Life. We have no power over the past and we do not know the future. As far as the future is concerned we have but these three certitudes, but we possess a fourth in this very moment, and that fourth is all: it is that of our actuality, of our present liberty to choose God and thus to choose our whole destiny. In this instant, this present, we hold our whole life, our whole existence: all is good if this instant is good, and if we know how to fix our life in this hallowed instant; all the secret of spiritual faithfulness lies in dwelling in this instant, in renewing it and perpetuating it by prayer, in holding on to it by means of the spiritual rhythm, in enclosing wholly within it the time that floods over us and threatens to drag us far away from this "divine moment". The vocation of the monk is perpetual prayer, not because life is long, but because it is only a moment; the perpetuity—or the rhythm—of the orison demonstrates that life is but an ever-present instant, just as the spatial fixation in a consecrated place demonstrates that the world is but a point, a point however which belongs to God, and is therefore everywhere and excludes no bliss.

This condensation of the existential dimensions—in so far as they are indefinite and arbitrary—into a hallowed unity is at the same time the very thing that constitutes the essence of man; the rest is contingency and accident. This is a truth that concerns every human being; the monk too is not a being apart, but simply a prototype or a model, or a spiritual specification, a landmark: every man, because he is a man, should realise in one way or another this victory over a world that disperses and over a life that enslaves. Too many people think that they have not time to pray, but this is an illusion due to that indifference which is, according to Fénélon, the worst sickness of the soul; for the many moments we fill with our habitual dreams, including our all too often useless reflections, we take away from God and from ourselves.

The great mission of monasticism is to show to the world that happiness does not lie somewhere far away, or in something situated outside ourselves, in a treasure to be sought or in a world to be built, but here where we belong to God. The monk represents, in face of a dehumanized world, what our true standards are; his mission is to remind men what man is.

NOTES

(1) "For what is a man profited, if he shall gain the whole world, and lose his own soul?" (Matt. xvi. 26).

(2) "Be fruitful, and multiply, and replenish the earth, and subdue it; and have dominion over the fish of the sea, and over the fowl of the air, and over every living thing that moveth upon the earth." (Genesis i. 28).

(3) The partisans of this "forcing into step" must be answered by the Scriptures; "Whoso therefore will be a friend of the world is the enemy of God." (James iv. 4.) "And be not conformed to this world: but be ye transformed by the renewing of your mind, that ye may prove what is that good, and acceptable, and perfect, will of God." (Rom. xii. 2.) In our days it is the other way round: it is atheistic scientism, it is demagogy, it is the machine that decides what is good, what should be pleasing to God, what is perfect. "Woe unto you, when all men shall speak well of you! for so did their fathers to the false prophets." (Luke vi. 26.) "Love not the world, neither the things that are in the world. If any man love the world, the love of the Father is not in him." (I John ii. 16.) And St. Francis of Sales addresses the human soul in these words: "God did not put you into this world because of any need that he had of you, who are quite useless to him, but only that he might exercise in you his goodness, giving you his grace and his glory. To this end he has given you understanding wherewith to know him, memory wherewith to remember him, will wherewith to love him, imagination that you might picture his benefits, eyes that you might see the marvels of his works, a tongue wherewith to praise him, and likewise with the other faculties. Being created and put into this world with that intention, all intentions contrary thereto must be rejected and avoided, and those that in no way serve this end must be despised as being vain and superfluous. Consider the misfortune of the world which thinks not at all of this, but lives as if thinking that it had been created only to build houses, plant trees, amass riches and disport itself." (*Introduction to the Devout Life*, Chapter X.)

CHAPTER IX

RELIGIO PERENNIS

ONE of the keys to the understanding of our true nature and of our ultimate destiny is the fact that the things of this world never measure up to the real range of our intelligence. Our intelligence is made for the Absolute, or it is nothing. Among all the intelligences of this world the human spirit alone is capable of objectivity, and this implies—or proves—that what confers on our intelligence the power to accomplish to the full what it can accomplish, and what makes it wholly what it is, is the Absolute alone.[1] If it were necessary or useful to prove the Absolute, the objective and transpersonal character of the human intellect would be sufficient as evidence, for that same intellect testifies irrecusably to a purely spiritual first Cause, to a Unity infinitely central but containing all things, to an Essence at once immanent and transcendent. It has been said more than once that total Truth is inscribed, in an immortal script, in the very substance of our spirit; what the different Revelations do is to "crystallize" and "actualize", in different degrees according to the case, a nucleus of certitudes which not only abides forever in the divine Omniscience, but also sleeps by refraction in the "naturally supernatural" kernel of the individual, as well as in that of each ethnic or historical collectivity or of the human species as a whole.

Similarly, in the case of the will, which is no more than a prolongation or a complement of the intelligence: the objects which it commonly sets out to achieve, or those which life imposes on it, do not match up to the fulness of its range; the "divine dimension" alone can satisfy the thirst for plenitude of our willing, or of our love. What makes our will human, and therefore free, is the fact that it is proportioned to God;

in God alone it is kept free from all constraint, and thus from everything that limits its nature.

The essential function of human intelligence is discernment between the Real and the illusory, or between the Permanent and the impermanent, and the essential function of the will is attachment to the Permanent or to the Real. This discernment and this attachment are the quintessence of all spirituality. Carried to their highest level, or reduced to their purest substance, they constitute the underlying universality in every great spiritual patrimony of humanity, or what may be called the *religio perennis*.[2] This and nothing else is the religion of the sages, but always and necessarily on a foundation of divinely instituted formal elements.[3]

*   *   *

Metaphysical discernment is a "separation" between *Ātmā* and *Māyā*; contemplative concentration, or a unifying consciousness, is on the other hand a "union" of *Māyā* with *Ātmā*. Discernment is separative[4] and is what "doctrine" is concerned with; concentration is unitive and is what "method" is concerned with; "faith" is related to the first element, and the "love of God" to the second.

The *religio perennis* is fundamentally this, to paraphrase the well-known saying of St. Irenaeus: the Real entered into the illusory so that the illusory might be able to return into the Real. It is this mystery, together with the metaphysical discernment and contemplative concentration that are its complement, which alone is important in an absolute sense from the point of view of gnosis. For the gnostic (in the etymological and rightful sense of that word) there is in the last analysis no other religion. It is what Ibn Arabi called the "religion of love", putting the accent on the element of "realization".

The two-fold definition of the *religio perennis*, discernment between the Real and the illusory, and a unifying and permanent concentration on the Real—implies in addition the criteria of intrinsic orthodoxy for every religion and all spirituality. In order to be orthodox a religion must possess a mythological or doctrinal symbolism establishing the essential distinction in question, and must offer a way that secures both the perfection of concentration and also its continuity. In other words a religion is orthodox on condition that it offers a sufficient, if not always exhaustive, idea of the absolute and the relative, and therewith an idea of their reciprocal relationships, and also a spiritual activity that is contemplative in its nature and effectual as concerns our ultimate destiny. It is notorious that heterodoxies always tend to adulterate either the idea of the divine Principle or the manner of our attachment to it; they offer either a worldly, profane or, if you like, "humanist" counterfeit of religion, or else a mysticism with a content of nothing but the *ego* and its illusions.

*　　*　　*

To treat of a subject as complex as that of spiritual perspectives in simple and as it were schematic terms might be held to indicate lack of sense of proportion, but since the very nature of things allows an aspect of simplicity to be taken into account, the truth would be no better served by following the meanders of a complexity not called for in this case. Analysis is one function of the intelligence, and synthesis is another; the common association of the idea of intelligence with that of difficulty, or of the idea of facility with that of presumption, has evidently no relation to the true nature of the Intellect. Intellectual vision has something in common with optical vision: there are things that must be examined in detail if they are to be understood, and others that are more clearly perceived from a certain distance, when the resultant simplification conveys their real nature all the more clearly. Truth can expand and differentiate indefinitely, but it is also contained in a "geometrical point"; the whole thing is to grasp this point, whatever the symbol or the symbolism that in fact brings about the act of intellection.

Truth is one, and it would be vain to refuse to look for it except in one particular place, for the Intellect contains in its substance all that is true, so that truth cannot but be manifested wherever the Intellect is deployed in the atmosphere of a Revelation. Space can be represented by a circle as well as by a cross, a spiral, a star or a square; and just as it is impossible that there should be only one figure to represent the nature of space or of extension, so also it is impossible that there should be only one doctrine giving an account of the Absolute and of the relations between the contingent and the Absolute. In other words, a belief that there can only be one true doctrine is comparable to a denial of the plurality of the figures used to indicate the characteristics of space, or, to choose a very different example, to a denial of the plurality of individual consciousnesses and visual points of view. In each Revelation God says "I" while placing Himself extrinsically at a point of view other than that of earlier Revelations, hence the appearance of contradiction on the plane of formal crystallization.

The objection might perhaps be raised that the various geometrical figures are not strictly equivalent in their capacity to reconcile graphic symbolism with spatial extension, and that therefore the comparison just made could also be used as an argument against the equivalence of traditional perspectives. The answer to this objection is that traditional perspectives are not meant so much to provide precise representations, at least *a priori*, as to be ways of salvation and means of deliverance. And in any case, granted that the circle—not even to mention the point—is a more direct representation of space by form than is the cross or any other differentiated figure, and that therefore the circle reflects more perfectly the nature of extension, there is still this to be considered : the cross, the square or the spiral express explicitly a spatial reality which the circle or the point express only implicitly. The differentiated figures are therefore irreplaceable, otherwise they would not exist, and they are in no sense various kinds of imperfect circles; the cross is infinitely nearer to the perfection of the point or of the circle than are the oval or the trapezoid, for example. Analogous considerations apply to traditional doctrines, as concerns their differences of form and their efficacy in equating the contingent to the Absolute.

*   *   *

And now let us return to our *religio perennis*, envisaged either as metaphysical discernment and unifying concentration, or as the descent of the divine Principle which becomes manifestation in order that manifestation may return to the Principle.

In Christianity, according to St. Irenaeus, God "became man" so that man might "become God". In Hindu terms one would say: *Ātmā* became *Māyā* so that *Māyā* might become *Ātmā*. In Christianity, contemplative and unifying concentration means dwelling in the manifested Real, in the "Word made flesh", so that this Real may dwell in us, who are illusory, according to what Christ said in a vision of St. Catherine of Siena: "I am He who is, thou art she who is not". The soul dwells in the Real, in the Kingdom of God that is "within us", by virtue of the permanent prayer of the heart, as is taught by the parable of the unjust judge and by St. Paul's injunction to pray without ceasing.

In Islam the same theme, fundamental because it is universal, is crystallized according to a very different point of view. Discernment between the Real and the unreal is affirmed by the Testimony of the Unity (the Shahādah); the correlative concentration on the Symbol, or the permanent consciousness of the Real, is effected through this same Testimony or through the divine Name that synthesizes it and is thus the quintessential crystallization of the Koranic Revelation. This Testimony or this Name is also the quintessence of the Revelation of Abraham, through the lineage of Ishmael, and goes back to the Semitic branch of the primordial Revelation. The Real "descended" (*nazzala, unzila*), it entered into the non-real or the illusory, the "perishable" (*fānin*)[5] in becoming the *Qur-'an*—or the *Shahādah* which summarizes it, or the *Ism* (the "Name") which is its auditive and graphic essence, or the *Dhikr* (the "Mention") which is its operative synthesis—in order that on this divine bark the illusory might return to the Real, to the "Countenance (*Wajh*) of the Lord which alone abides" (*Wa yabqā Wajhu Rabbika*),[6] whatever be the metaphysical compass attributed to the ideas of "illusion" and of "Reality". In this reciprocity lies all the mystery of the "Night of Destiny" (*Laylat al-Qadr*), which is a "descent", and of the "Night of Ascension" (*Laylat al-Mi'rāj*) which is the complementary phase; contemplative realization, or "unification" (*tawhīd*), partakes of this ascension of the Prophet through the degrees of Paradise. "Verily (says the Koran) prayer guards against the major (*fahshā*) and the minor (*munkar*) sins, but the mention (*dhikr*) of *Allāh* is greater".[7]

Nearer to the Christian perspective in a certain connection, but much more remote in another, is the Buddhist perspective, which on the one hand is based on a "Word made flesh", but on the other knows nothing of the anthropomorphic notion of a God who is Creator. In Buddhism the two terms of the alternative, or of discernment, are *Nirvāna*, the Real, and *Samsāra*, the illusory. The way is in the last analysis the permanent consciousness of *Nirvāna* in its aspect as *Shūnya*, the "Void", or else it is concentration on the saving manifestation of *Nirvāna*, the Buddha, who is *Shūnyamūrti*, "Manifestation of the Void". In the Buddha, notably in his form *Amitābha*, *Nirvāna* became *Samsāra* so that *Samsāra* might become *Nirvāna*; and if *Nirvāna* is the Real and *Samsāra* is illusion, the *Buddha* is the Real in the illusory and the *Bodhisattva* is the illusory in the Real;[8] this suggests the symbolism of the Yin-Yang. The passage from the illusory to the Real is described in the *Prajñā-Pāramitā-Hridaya-Sūtra* in these terms: "Gone, gone, gone towards the far shore, landed on the far shore, O Illumination, be blessed!"

*   *   *

Every spiritual outlook must in the nature of things confront a conception of man with a corresponding conception of God. Hence arise three ideas or three definitions concerning firstly, man himself, secondly, God as He reveals Himself to man when man is defined in such and such a way, and thirdly, man as determined and transformed by God in terms of the outlook in question.

From the point of view of human subjectivity man is the container and God is the contained; from the divine point of view (if any such expression be allowable) the relationship is reversed, all things being contained in God and nothing being able to contain Him. The statement that man is made in the image of God includes the implication that God takes on himself, *a posteriori* and as far as man is concerned, something of that image; God is pure Spirit and man is consequently intelligence or consciousness; inversely, if man is defined as intelligence, God appears as "Truth". In other words, God, desiring to affirm Himself in His aspect of "Truth", addresses Himself to man in so far as man is endowed with intelligence, just as He addresses Himself to man in distress to affirm His Mercy, or to man endowed with free will to affirm Himself as the Law that brings salvation.

The "proofs" of God and of religion are in man himself. "Knowing his own nature, he also knows Heaven" says Mencius, in agreement with other analogous and well-known maxims. We must extract from the material of our own nature the key certitude that opens up the way to a certitude of the divine and of Revelation; the very word "man" implies "God", the very word "relative" implies "Absolute". Human nature in general and human intelligence in particular cannot be understood apart from the phenomenon of religion, which characterizes them in the most direct and the most complete way possible. If we can grasp the transcendent nature (not the "psychological" nature) of the human being, we thereby grasp the nature of revelation, of religion, of tradition; we understand their possibility, their necessity, their truth. And in understanding religion, not only in a particular form or according to some verbal specification, but also in its formless essence, we understand the religions, that is to say, the meaning of their plurality and their diversity; this is the plane of gnosis, of the *religio perennis*, whereon the extrinsic antinomies of dogma are explained and resolved.

*   *   *

On the outward and therefore contingent plane, which however inevitably has its importance in the human order, there is a concordance between the *religio perennis* and virgin nature, and by the same token between it and primordial nudity, the nudity of creation, of birth, of resurrection, or that of the High Priest in the Holy of Holies, of a hermit in the desert,[9] of a Hindu *sadhu* or *sanyasi*, of a Red Indian in silent prayer on a mountain.[10] Nature inviolate is at once a vestige of the Earthly Paradise and a prefiguration of the Heavenly Paradise; sanctuaries and costumes differ, but virgin nature and the human body remain faithful to the initial unity. The function of sacred art, which seems to tend away from that unity, is in reality only that of reinstating natural phenomena as vehicles of divine messages to which men have become insensible; in art the perspective of love tends towards overflowing and profusion, whereas the perspective of gnosis tends towards nature, simplicity and silence; this is represented by the contrast between the richness of the Gothic and the sparingness of Zen.[11] But this must not lead us to lose sight of the fact that external frameworks or modes are always contingent, and that all combinations and all compensations are possible, just as in spirituality all possibilities can be reflected one in another, according to their appropriate modalities.

A civilization is integrated and healthy to the extent that it is founded on the "invisible" or "underlying" religion, the *religio perennis*; that is to say, to the extent that its expressions or its forms are transparent to the Formless and are turned towards the Origin, thus providing a vehicle for the recollection of a lost Paradise, but also, and with all the more reason, for the presentiment of a timeless Beatitude. For the Origin is at once within us and before us; time is but a spiroidal movement around a motionless Centre.

NOTES

(1) "Neither in the earth nor in the heavens is there room for Me (Allāh) but in the heart of My believing servant there is room for Me" (*hadīth qudsi*). Similarly Dante: "I perceive that our intellect is never satisfied, if the True does not enlighten it, outside which no truth is possible". (Paradiso III, 124–126.)

(2) These words recall the *philosophia perennis* of Steuchus Eugubin (sixteenth century) and of the neo-scholastics; but the word "philosophia" suggests rightly or wrongly a mental elaboration rather than wisdom, and therefore does not convey exactly the intended sense.

Religio is that which "binds" (*religat*) man to Heaven and engages his whole being; as for the word "*traditio*", it is related to a more outward and sometimes fragmentary reality, besides suggesting a retrospective outlook. At its birth a religion "binds" men to Heaven from the moment of its first revelation, but it does not become a "tradition", or admit more than one "tradition", till two or three generations later.

(3) This is true even in the case of the pre-Islamic Arab sages, who lived spiritually on the heritage of Abraham and Ishmael.

(4) This is what the Arabic word *furqān* signifies, namely, "qualitative differentiation", from *faraqa,* to separate, to discern, to bifurcate. It is well known that *Furqān* is one of the names of the Koran.

(5) The word *fanā*, sometimes translated as "extinction" by analogy with the Sanscrit *nirvāna*, has the same root, and really means "perishable nature".

(6) Koran, Surat of the Merciful, 27.

(7) Koran, Surat of the Spider, 45.

(8) See *Les Mystere du Bodhisattva* by F. Schuon (Etudes Traditionnelles, 11 Quai St. Michel, Paris, Nos. 371 and 372–373).

(9) Such as Mary the Egyptian, in whose case the "formless" and wholly inward character of a love controlled by God partakes of the qualities of gnosis, so much so that one could call it a "gnosis of love" (in the sense of *parabhakti*).

(10) Simplicity of clothing and its colour, white in particular, sometimes replace the symbolism of nudity in the art of clothing. On every plane, the laying bare that is inspired by the naked Truth counterbalances a worldly "culturism". But in other connections the sacred robe symbolizes the victory of the Spirit over the flesh, and then its hieratic richness, which it would be a great mistake to look upon with disfavour, expresses the inexhaustible profusion of the Mystery and of Glory.

(11) But it is evident that the most sumptuous sacred art is infinitely nearer to gnosis than the ignorant and affected "sparingness" of those of our contemporaries who profess to be "making a clean sweep". Only a simplicity that is qualitative, noble, and conformable to the essence of things reflects and transmits the perfume of a supra-formal wisdom.